Dividend Growth Whisperer

Shane Forbes is a retired investment actuary and former Fellow of the Society of Actuaries. He holds an Honors Bachelor's degree, First Class (*summa cum laude*), in Mathematics and Physics from Dalhousie University, Halifax, Canada, and a Master's degree in Mathematics from the University of Toronto, Toronto, Canada. *Dividend Growth Whisperer* is his third book. His other books are:

- *Investing in Dividend Growth Stocks*, print edition

- *Investing in Dividend Growth Stocks*, digital edition, a substantially expanded edition of the print edition

Dividend Growth Whisperer

A Short And Sweet Guide To Understanding And
Profiting From Your Best Long-Term Investment

Shane Forbes

NeoCadence LLC

November 2018

NeoCadence LLC
Web: www.neocadence.com
Email: publishing@neocadence.com
Mail: PO Box 338, Gotha FL 34734

First print edition published November 2018 (copies may include the printing date and location on the last page).

ISBN (print edition) 978-0-9822870-3-3

In memory of my parents, Arlene and Russel Forbes.

Historical point-in-time stock price data retrieved from SEC filings. Historical time-series stock price data obtained from QUANDL.

IMPORTANT: Investment opinion is not investment advice. This book reflects the Author's opinion. It is not investment advice. The Author and Publisher are not financial advisors. Please speak to a financial advisor or other appropriate professional who understands your situation before investing in the instruments mentioned in this book. Investing in the financial markets, including the stock market, and in particular the instruments mentioned in this book, entails risk. Be mindful of the risks involved. The Author and Publisher are not responsible for any losses that may be incurred and in particular expressly disclaim any liability that may be incurred from investing in the investments mentioned in this book or from following the methods in this book. This book primarily pertains to U.S. securities and U.S. markets. It may not be relevant to other securities and other markets. This book provides links to sites on the web, retrieved as of mid-2018. The Author and Publisher are not responsible if the addresses of these sites change and are not responsible for the content of these sites. This book includes a link to an Excel 2007 spreadsheet. The spreadsheet comes with no warranties, implied or otherwise. The Author and Publisher are not responsible for any losses that may be incurred, and in particular expressly disclaim any liability that may be incurred, on using this spreadsheet. Use at your own risk.

Contents

Prelude to Chapter 2   29

31 | 2. TUESDAY – THE NUMBERS AS CONFIRMATION

Prelude to Chapter 3   47

49 | 3. WEDNESDAY – STRONG RETURNS

Preface

"*Every living thing must grow. It can't stand still. It must grow or perish.*"

Ayn Rand (Atlas Shrugged)

Among the many thousands of possible investments and hundreds of possible investment strategies, few really work, and by really work, I mean generate good returns – over the long term – with relatively low risk. A dividend growth investment strategy is one of the best, if not the best, strategy for the typical investor.

Why? The math simply works. With these stocks, the math – from the company's business to its appraisal in the stock market to the returns that the investor earns – simply works. With most other stocks, the math does not work – something along the line breaks, ruining your returns.

In *Dividend Growth Whisperer*, I distill the very essence of dividend growth stocks. The book is short, gets to the point, and can make you a virtual expert in less than a week.

Written for the intelligent investor, *Dividend Growth Whisperer* comprises six chapters, the first five requiring an hour or so of your time except for the last chapter which should take two:

- In Chapter 1, *Traits of a Good (Long-Term) Business*, the book establishes the key qualitative aspects to look for in a long-term business, dividend growth stocks arising from the universe of good long-term businesses. Most businesses fail. There's a reason for this.

- In Chapter 2, *The Numbers as Confirmation*, you will learn about the quantitative signs of a good business. Numbers matter. Management often gilds their company's performance. Unless entombed in outright fraught, the numbers do not lie. But which numbers matter? Not all. A few do. And one is crucial.

- Next, the book segues to the investor. In Chapter 3, *Strong Returns*, it asks, What are the constituents of an investor's return? The chapter connects you, the investor, to the business. The stock market functions as the intermediary.

- In Chapter 4, *Prospecting for Stalwarts*, the book shows you how to find high-quality dividend growth stocks. High-quality dividend growth stocks are a select few, numbering fewer than a 100 or so – out of 15,000+ stocks. Blindly throwing darts will not work.

- After finding your stalwarts, you must estimate what return you can expect. I cannot stress this enough. Operating blindly in this regard can decimate your returns – for instance, popular stocks not always generating the best returns. In Chapter 5, *The Right Kind of Magic*, I present an entirely original method, a genuine piece of magic, if I may be so bold, that will answer the final question, What return should you expect?

- But of what good is talk in and of itself? In Chapter 6, *Examples*, I present a plethora of examples of very strong dividend growth stocks. Each is studied carefully and thoroughly. And each includes the long-term return that you can expect. As a bonus, the chapter shows you how to value a dividend growth fund and the stock market itself. The stock market is certainly not a bargain these days!

But wait, there's more. This book also includes a useful *checklist* that you can use to evaluate *any* dividend growth stock and concludes with the *seven keys* to help make you a top-notch dividend growth investor, a dividend growth *whisperer*, so to speak.

In one week, a few hours of careful reading, you should be set and ready to go.

Prelude to Chapter 1

"The investor of today does not profit from yes-
terday's growth."   *Warren Buffett*

Never accept the dogma that a company's dividend growth is somehow automatic, that looking at a company's dividend history somehow "confirms" the future. History has proved many such "confirmations" wrong.

Instead, as we shall see, *dividend growth results – ultimately – from a good (long-term) business and a stable and moderate company (and underlying market) growth rate.* Take these away and dividend growth suffers.

A good business is a given (though many dividend growth books fail to define, or even consider, what constitutes a good business). In Chapter 1, we begin our journey by studying *the traits of a good (long-term) business, the most important of which is being in a market with no more than a reasonable level of competition.*

With a reasonable level of competition, the company enjoys reasonable profits. What companies do with these profits is (a) invest internally, or externally, theoretically earning a very healthy return; (b) retain some for adverse times; and (c) pay shareholders something reasonable. In effect, reasonable competition allows companies to make enough for themselves *and* their shareholders.

But will these profits grow? If not, take a pass on the investing train – your investment returns will suffer.

In fact, successful dividend growth *requires* that the company generate (1) stable and (2) modestly growing profits. (1) Stability means that the company's results do not fluctuate too much. Stability of the business, thus profits, accords companies a view into the future, allowing them to comfortably plan for a growing dividend. Stability is also crucial for *you*, the long-term investor. Stable profits imply that the stock price does not bounce around too much, *helping you remain invested, absolutely crucial for generating strong long-term returns – as, generally speaking, the more exposed you are to the market over the long term, the better you will do.* (2) Moderate growth is necessary because – with slow growth – dividends do not grow and returns can be anemic, while with fast growth, competition is rife and long-term company performance tends to suffer. *Likewise, as a successful long-term investor, you will find that modest growth is the only growth that matters.* Fast growth peters out, the stock price eventually cratering; slow growth never amounts to much, the stock price stuck at neutral.

To summarize, here is your first dividend growth lesson: **Look for stable (or, even better, falling) competition and stable, modestly growing profits.** ♣

1. Monday – Traits of A Good (Long-Term) Business

"My own business always bores me to death; I prefer other people's."   Oscar Wilde

The long and dazzling dividend histories of companies such as Fannie Mae and Freddie Mac led many an investor astray. They believed that these businesses – and their dividends and dividend growth – would endure.

Yet, up against an economic maelstrom in 2008, these businesses were tested and put to the sword. These – and others like them – collapsed. Dividends were reduced. Dividends were obliterated. Even today, mid-2018, many remain just a pale shadow of what they once were.

In the meantime, in the midst of market pandemonium and fear, other companies continued to prosper. On 12 September 2008, Abbott announced its 339th consecutive dividend. Thirteen days later, McDonald's announced a 33 percent increase in its dividend.

> For companies such as Abbott and McDonald's, *the vitality of dividends springs from the vigor of fortress-like businesses, businesses that through the economy's ups and downs generate the strong and steady profits that support rich and rising dividends.*

Companies respond to the state of the economy, the economy at any point in time being steady, strong, or weak.

- In steady economies, good businesses grow. They implement their business plans. They grow at an even and controlled pace. They pay steadily rising dividends.

- In strong economies, cheap capital gives weak businesses a toehold. But economies do not remain strong forever – the good times do not last.

- When the bad times come, as they invariably do, weak businesses suffer, or fold. Strong businesses, however, persist.

Dividend growth companies, the strong businesses that they are, survive the bad times, grow a bit above long-term trend during the strong times, and grow at their long-term average during the steady times. They persist. They do not fade away. Their dividends and returns compound, their long-term investors becoming incredibly rich.

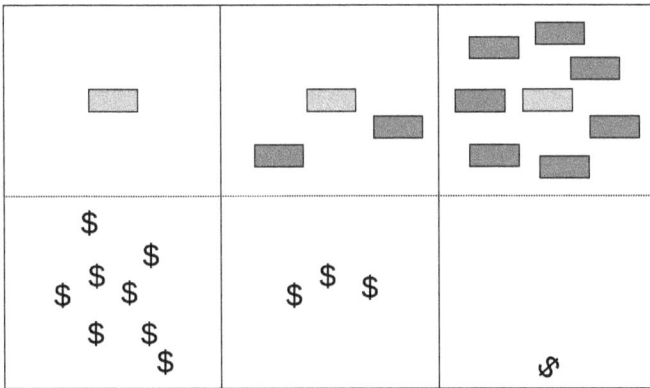

Figure 1.1: Extreme competition leads to collapsing profits.

COMPETITION

"Competition is a sin." John D. Rockefeller

> **What is the competition? Ask that first of all of your long-term investments.** I cannot stress this enough. Competition erodes the vitality of a business. Without competition, investing would be simple – companies would act like monopolies and shareholders would reap their dividends.

The fewer the number of competitors, the better. Ideally, look for businesses where two competitors share a large percentage, (say) 80 percent, of a growing market. One competitor with 80 percent is even better, though such instances are rare.

In fact, few companies enjoy the comfort of none or limited competition. On the contrary, most companies face a Darwinian struggle to survive. Though a company may experience little competition at first, as new competition emerges, sales growth starts to weaken, profit growth starts to slow. *Competition is like friction – the more of it there is, the less freely you move.* With extreme competition, profits collapse (Figure 1.1).

A seemingly perennially troubled hyper-competitive industry is passenger aviation. With seats often seemingly plentiful, airlines compete primarily on price. Moreover, airline costs are tied to rigid labor deals and the volatile price of oil. As a result, with excessive pricing pressure and high and inflexible costs, airline profits vary *wildly*. Airlines go in and – if they are fortunate – out of bankruptcy, though, of late, to be fair, because of consolidation, the industry seems to have improved, though in turn, this very likely means new competitors will emerge, ruining the profitability of this messy industry once again.

Even Warren Buffett does not always get it right. In 1989, he bought $358 million of preferred stock in USAir. He sold his position at an overall profit eight years later – but it was an unusually difficult and bumpy ride.

Quoting from Berkshire Hathaway's 1996 Chairman's Letter:

> When Richard Branson, the wealthy owner of Virgin Atlantic Airways, was asked how to become a millionaire, he had a quick answer: "There's really nothing to it. Start as a billionaire and then buy an airline." Unwilling to accept Branson's proposition on faith, your Chairman decided in 1989 to test it by investing $358 million in a 9.25% preferred stock of USAir.

> I liked and admired Ed Colodny, the company's then-CEO, and I still do. But my analysis of USAir's business was both superficial and wrong. I was so beguiled by the company's long history of profitable operations, and by the protection that ownership of a senior security seemingly offered me, that I overlooked the crucial point: USAir's revenues would increasingly feel the effects of an unregulated, fiercely-competitive market whereas its cost structure was a holdover from the days when regulation protected profits. These costs, if left unchecked, portended disaster, however reassuring the airline's past record might be. (If history supplied all of the answers, the Forbes 400 would consist of librarians.) [The problem with history here relates to dividend history as well. Just because a company has paid a growing dividend in the past does not mean it can do so in the future.]

> To rationalize its costs, however, USAir needed major improvements in its labor contracts – and that's something

most airlines have found it extraordinarily difficult to get, short of credibly threatening, or actually entering, bankruptcy. USAir was to be no exception. Immediately after we purchased our preferred stock, the imbalance between the company's costs and revenues began to grow explosively. In the 1990-1994 period, USAir lost an aggregate of $2.4 billion, a performance that totally wiped out the book equity of its common stock.

New competition brings in new technology and a different way of doing things. Established companies are often set in their ways. Instead of adapting to change, they often persist in denial. Blockbuster faced years of growing competition from Netflix – and years of denial – before the reality of its fate set in. The company declared bankruptcy in 2010. Whereas once the company had more than 9,000 stores worldwide, today it survives as a crust of its former self. As of mid-2018, it has no corporate U.S. stores. Just *one* franchised U.S. store remains – in Bend, Oregon. This store has become somewhat of a tourist attraction. From an article in the Washington Post, "Tourists flock to the city nestled outside the Deschutes National Forest, eager to get selfies with the Blockbuster sign. Some even stop in to buy something, she said."

High profits attract competition. When profits are high, new competition emerges. In time, the market becomes oversupplied. Pricing becomes irrational. Profits collapse.

High growth attracts competition. During the Internet boom of the late 1990s, competition bubbled. Virtually everyone wanted in. With extreme competition, the market broke. Profits tumbled. Companies collapsed. Even for the survivors, the road back has been long. And painful. Lucent, later a part of Alcatel-Lucent, and now a part of Nokia, has never really recovered. Sun was bought out by Oracle. Cisco has tried to adapt – and, as of mid-2018, its stock price has climbed out of a long morass – but it will take many more years before it broaches its Year 2000 (!) high.

Some countries view their commodity semiconductor makers as essential to their economies. When these companies get into difficulty, the governments step in to provide support. As a result, the industry never sheds its weakest players. Yet, without a regular pruning of the weakest, an industry can get distorted.

In general, *avoid investing in companies that face rising competition*. With rising competition, a company sees declining internal returns. In time, your returns will do the same. In general, *you will do your portfolio an immense amount of good if you invest in companies that face stable or falling competition*. With stable competition, if the company's internal returns are already high, they are more likely to remain that way – at a minimum. With falling competition, the company's internal returns are more likely to increase – and your returns will do the same.

Ideally, a high-quality established business – the type of business exemplified by the typical dividend growth stock – shares the following overriding competitive traits, traits that suggest stable or falling competition:

- The company has few competitors and competitors act rationally. In a perfect world (for its shareholders), the company dominates its markets, for instance, by virtue of its size.

- The business produces profits that are good but not necessarily obscene. Obscene profits attract competition.

- The business grows at a pace that isn't hurried (but also isn't soporific). High growth attracts competition. In the early 2000s, internet-related companies found this out the hard way.

- The company's markets are expensive to enter but easy to exit. Passenger aviation is a counterexample to the expensive to enter requirement. Commodity semiconductors are a counterexample to the easy to exit requirement.

BUSINESS STABILITY

> *Stable, modestly growing profits form the basis of dividend growth*. Profits should not vary wildly, like a yo-yo, from year to year. A company with wildly varying profits cannot hope to pay a dividend, let alone a growing dividend. Ideally, profits grow modestly from year to year and never vary wildly.

The consumer staples sector exemplifies the type of stability we hope to see with our dividend growth stocks (however, many of these stocks lack growth – that's another matter, which we will get to in due time). Because businesses in the consumer staples sector sell *inexpensive and recurring products*, demand does not collapse when the economy slows. Moreover, demand growth is steady.

By contrast, unless they have offsets such as a strong brand or a dominant market position, companies that sell expensive things (for instance, houses) or occasional things (for instance, fads) can never be good dividend-paying stocks. Profits vary too widely, as with houses, or eventually flop, as with fads.

Diversification aids stability. Diversification reduces business risks and helps control costs. For instance, a company with operations in many countries faces reduced currency risks. Likewise, a company with many suppliers pays less for its raw materials.

Generally, large companies are more stable than small companies:

- Large companies have more pricing power.

- They can more easily influence their suppliers.

- They can market widely, persistently, and aggressively.

- They can raise funds more easily – and at better prices.

- They can more readily absorb legal and other business risks.

- They are less likely to lose money when business stalls because they more readily cover their *fixed costs*. By contrast, when business stalls, many small companies quickly slide into the red. (Businesses face two types of costs: *fixed costs* and *variable costs*. Fixed costs do not vary with how many items are produced; variable costs do. Rent is a fixed cost; the cost of raw materials to produce what a business sells is a variable cost.)

Stability helps companies survive. Stable businesses have a reasonable idea of what the next quarter and next year will bring. Growth is neither excessive nor negative. **Stable companies persist, an essential trait of any investment if you want to be a long-term owner.** For instance, Nestlé, the consumer staples giant, has been around since 1866. Yes, 1866, one year after the U.S. Civil War ended.

GROWTH

"You've got to do your own growing, no matter how tall your grandfather was." Irish Saying

As companies age, they travel along a well-cobbled path (Figure 1.2). The *successful* company grows from embryonic stage to small-cap to midcap to large-cap. Sales grow slowly, then rapidly, then moderate, then crawl. Earnings, that is, the company's profits, can vary dramatically because companies differ widely in how they control their costs. Still, over a successful company's lifetime, it should have minted its early investors fortunes.

The investment path mirrors the growth path. The successful company progresses from speculative stock to aggressive growth stock to growth stock to dividend growth stock to conservative stock, where, by conservative stock, I mean the company finds few areas to invest, thus grows slowly, but compensates shareholders with a high dividend payout.

The dividend growth stage differs from the earlier stages by how much cash the company generates. During the earliest stages, the company – like a child that depends on its parents – depends on outside funds to grow. It does not grow so rapidly otherwise. As time progresses, and the company gets larger, growth begins to slow. At some point, the company begins to generate cash. Eventually, the company funds itself – effectively, the child is all grown up. *At the dividend growth stage, not only does the company fund itself, but it generates so much extra cash it can afford to pay dividends.*

This happy trajectory marks the successful company. But what of the company that is unsuccessful, either temporarily, or otherwise? Or, for that matter, what of the company that is temporarily too successful? Table 1.1 uses two variables, expected five-year earnings per share growth rate and company size, to delineate, *roughly – this can never be perfect as companies vary too much –* the possibilities for successful companies and others:

- The bold entries represent the typical successful company as it ages. Read it from bottom left to upper right – speculative to aggressive growth to growth; then across to growth, dividend growth; and so on.

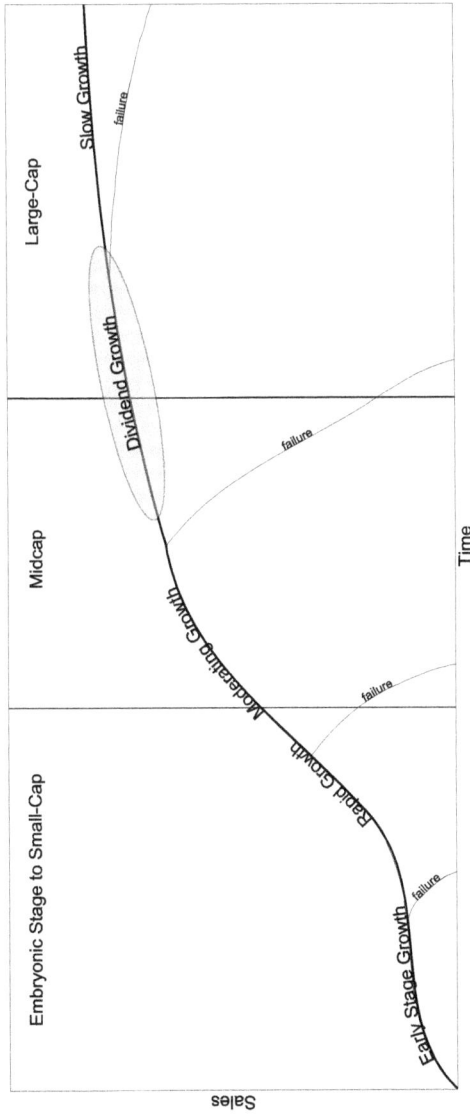

Figure 1.2: Stages of company growth. The growth rate changes as the company ages. Failure is a possibility at every stage.

Expected 5-year EPS growth rate	Company size		
	Small	Midsize	Large
Below 0%	Value	Value	Value
0-4%	Value	Value	Conservative
4-8%	Value	Conservative	**Conservative**
8-12%	Growth	**Growth, Div Gr**	**Growth, Div Gr**
12-16%	**Growth**	Growth, Div Gr	Agg Gr
16-20%	**Agg Gr**	Agg Gr	Speculative
Above 20%	**Speculative**	Speculative	Speculative

Table 1.1: Investing styles by expected five-year earnings per share (EPS) growth rate and company size. Aggr Gr stands for Aggressive Growth; Div Gr stands for Dividend Growth. For any company that sits on an overlapping expected five-year earnings per share growth rate boundary, place the company in the slot you deem fit.

- The cells above the topmost bold entries that do *not* say "value" represent companies that are slightly less successful than their bold (successful) counterparts.

- The cells above the topmost bold entries that say "value" correspond to companies that are unsuccessful, temporarily or otherwise.

- The cells below the bottommost bold entries correspond to companies that are temporarily *too* successful. Typically, few companies can sustain growth rates as high as these for long periods, (say) ten years or more.

(You may not be familiar with some of the terms above. Earnings per share is an accounting term, equal to the company's earnings, that is, its profits, divided by number of shares outstanding. Thus, if a company has earnings of $1,000 and 100 shares outstanding, its earnings per share is 1000 / 100 or $10. Growth rate, as always, is change – this period's value minus the prior period's value – divided by the prior period's value. Thus, a 10 percent earnings per share growth rate means earnings per share has grown from, (say) $20 to $22.)

In the table, company size refers to market capitalization. Market capitalization tells you how large a company is in the stock market.

Market capitalization is generally grouped as follows, at least as of mid-2018, though in this section I combine megacap and large-cap into large, and small and microcap (and below) into small:

- Megacap: $200 billion or more in market capitalization.

- Large-cap: between $10 billion and $199.9 billion in market capitalization.

- Midsize (or midcap): between $2 billion and $9.9 billion in market capitalization.

- Small-cap: between $300 million and $1.9 billion in market capitalization.

- Microcap (and below): less than $300 million in market capitalization.

In the table, the various combinations also correspond directly to various *investing styles*: speculative, aggressive growth, growth, dividend growth, conservative, and value. My characterization of "value" differs from commonly accepted definitions. I simply suggest that *something* has gone wrong, that the stock has taken a detour, deviating from the climbing, snaky path of the successful company depicted in Figure 1.2.

Of the twenty-one combinations, only three are suited to dividend growth:

- Midsize companies with expected five-year earnings per share growth rates of 8-12 percent a year;

- Midsize companies with expected five-year earnings per share growth rates of 12-16 percent a year; and

- Large companies with expected five-year earnings per share growth rates of 8-12 percent a year.

The company's *markets* and its competitive position within those markets drives this growth.

As a simple way of managing risk, mix and match stocks from the three combinations to suit your tolerance of risk. For instance, if you plan to buy twelve dividend growth stocks, but are cautious, choose (say) zero stocks of the first kind, zero of the second, and twelve of the third. If you are more adventurous, one or two chilies out of four, choose (say) two of the first kind, one of the second, and nine of the third. And so on.

> In Chapter 3, we will see that a company's earnings per share growth rate ultimately caps its dividend growth rate. *Thus, the above ranges for the earnings per share growth rate – 8-16 percent for a midsize company and 8-12 percent for a large company – ultimately cap the dividend growth rate for dividend growth stocks.*

MANAGEMENT

In today's global economy, read highly competitive economy, companies without quality leadership *will* stagnate or fail. But how do we determine quality? How do we differentiate the best managers from the pretenders?

Magazine listings are helpful. For instance, *Institutional Investor* runs an annual listing of the best CEOs in America, *Barron's* runs an annual listing of the *World's Most Respected Companies*, *Fortune* runs in-depth stories about companies and their managements.

Still, as useful as these listings can be, they are imperfect. In its 1995 list, *Fortune* ranked Enron 129th in its Fortune 500. In the 2002 list, Enron had risen to 5th. Flanking Enron were behemoths such as Ford and General Electric. It was an astonishing achievement.

It was also not real. Not long after the 2002 list was published, Enron filed for Chapter 11 bankruptcy protection. Enron's CEO, Kenneth Lay, and former CEO, Jeffrey Skilling, were convicted of fraud and conspiracy for lying to employees and investors. Lay died of a heart attack a few weeks after he was found guilty. Skilling was incarcerated for close to 14 years of a 24-year and 4-month sentence (his sentence was reduced). He was released to a halfway house in August 2018. Enron's CFO, Andrew Fastow, the architect behind the complex scheme, signed a plea agreement and testified against other executives. He served a 6-year prison sentence. Ironically, *Fortune* had even ranked Enron *America's Most Innovative Company*, not once, not twice, but *six years running*. Enron was certainly innovative, just not in a way the editors of *Fortune* could have foreseen.

Warren Buffett will not invest in a company if he does not believe in the quality of its management. Management pulls most of the strings. Management must be honest and capable with a track record that proves it. Without superior management, companies cannot succeed.

But how do we judge the quality of management? It isn't easy. Glowing financial results point the way – but sordid cases of fraud show that we cannot depend on financial results alone. We also have to rely on other incomplete – and imperfect – ways:

- Check that management has kept its word. Have managers done what they said they would do? *Do not invest in companies whose management continually finds excuses.*

- Does management keep the right perspective? Do they balance near-term profits with long-term investment? Or do they focus too much on the short term?

- On conference calls, is management well-reasoned? Or, conversely, impatient or hostile?

- Research management's track record. Did prior companies or divisions thrive under their stewardship? How fast did these prior companies or divisions grow?

- To get a feel for the company, its culture, and its management, read the CEO's letter to shareholders. Better yet, read several past letters as well.

- Management sets the standard for integrity. If management is dishonest, employees will follow. Gauge management's honesty during conference calls and presentations. Past behavior offers clues.

- Look for red flags such as insider sales and insider dealings. Both must be disclosed in filings with the SEC. Pay particular attention when many insiders sell suddenly and heavily. Among insider dealings that take place but should not:

  - Nepotism.
  - Loans to insiders.
  - Business transactions with entities that insiders own.

Lehman's CEO received hundreds of millions before the company collapsed. When companies are sold, they dole out golden handshakes. During retirement, it's annuities, life insurance, and health benefits. Some companies grant stock options *extremely* generously.

Excess pay and benefits add up – *when management (and employees) receive more than they are worth, when they gobble up too large a share of the pie, shareholders receive less than they deserve.*

SHAREHOLDER COMMITMENT: PAYING SHAREHOLDERS THEIR FAIR SHARE

In its company credo, Johnson & Johnson has this to say about its obligation to shareholders (stockholders):

> Our final responsibility is to our stockholders. Business must make a sound profit. We must experiment with new ideas. Research must be carried on, innovative programs developed and mistakes paid for. New equipment must be purchased, new facilities provided and new products launched. Reserves must be created to provide for adverse times. When we operate according to these principles, the stockholders should realize a fair return.

Shareholders own the business. They provide companies with funds. They do so directly when companies start up. They do so indirectly when they buy shares in the stock market. Shareholders expect a return on their funds.

Companies pay shareholders in three ways:

- They pay (cash) dividends, a direct way.

- They buy back shares, another direct way. When companies buy back shares, earnings per share typically rises. Share prices are more stubborn.

- They operate better, an indirect way. In theory, the stock market rewards better-run companies (that were not initially overvalued) with higher stock prices. Better operations underpin the first two ways. Better operations lead to higher profits. Higher profits lead to higher dividends and bigger share buybacks.

Dividends and share buybacks are also a function of the age and success of the company. Young companies need all their cash to grow. They cannot pay out much, if anything. Unsuccessful companies cannot pay out much, either. By contrast, more mature, successful companies, those exemplified by our dividend growth companies, can, and, more often than not, should.

Companies differ in how much they allocate between dividends and share buybacks. Some prefer the lower taxes and flexibility of share buybacks. Others value the explicit income that dividends provide.

Over the long term, and ideally, dividends per share grows and share count remains flattish or even falls. *As a rough guide – based entirely on the better stocks I have studied, so this is far from being a scientific sample – even with a reasonable dividend, share counts should fall 1-2 percent a year.* Companies should not pay out everything as dividends. Instead, they should compromise, preserving flexibility, with a reasonable dividend and a reasonable share buyback. Typically, share counts that fall three percent or more a year are ambitious – requiring that companies (not paying minuscule dividends or building up too much debt) earn rich internal returns. More often than not, dividends are low.

Some companies use debt to buy back shares. As debt changes a company's risk profile, debt must be manageable.

Always study a company's long-term history to determine if it has paid back shareholders fairly. Some companies have shareholder-friendly cultures. Others do not. Value Line provides a history of dividends and share counts.

BUSINESS RISKS

Companies, like trees subject to the whimsies of the weather, face a multitude of risks. Most relate to competition. Others relate to management. I covered competition and management earlier.

Another category of risks can bankrupt a company quickly. Be vigilant here. *Never* invest in a company with business risks so large that they can destroy it. For instance, a company may have a verdict go against it or it may not be able to refinance its debt or it may have had years of losses and does not have the financial strength to endure one more.

Companies list their business risks in the *Risk Factors* section of their annual reports – on Form 10-Ks – that they file with the SEC. Here are some of the more common – and important – business risks:

- State of the economy.

- Litigation. Be especially careful when a company indicates that a legal case can have a material adverse impact on its business.

- Size.

- Cyclicality – of the whole business or one or more of its parts.

- Lumpy sales. Steady sales are better than lumpy sales.

- Labor costs.

- Commodity costs.

- Lack of diversification, commonly in customers or suppliers.

- Damage to the company's brand. A respected brand allows a company to charge a premium.

- Pension and other benefit plans. These have costs, sometimes unexpected costs.

- Acquisitions. Acquisitions boost growth – but some do flop.

- Currency movements.

- Maturity of the business or industry.

- New competition.

- Lack of business vitality. Is the company's business in secular decline?

- Does the company sell to the U.S. government or other governments? Government budgets can be fickle.

- Is the company's business intrinsically volatile? For instance, a company that sells stock funds is vulnerable to movements in the stock market.

- Key individuals. Does the success of the business depend on a few key individuals?

- Excess insider ownership. Although some insider ownership is better than none, too much insider ownership spoils the broth. The insiders do as they please, often with little regard for other shareholders. Prada, as a company expense? Obviously.

If you are uncomfortable with a company's business risks, punt. There are always other choices, choices that are often separated by clean, hard numbers.

The numbers anchor hope to reality. They separate the stalwarts from the pretenders. In the next chapter, we turn to the numbers.

Quiz

1. The first question to ask of all of your long-term investments is what is the

    a) weather.
    b) meaning of life.
    c) competition.

2. High profits attract competition.

    a) True.
    b) False.

3. It is prudent to invest in a company that faces rising competition.

    a) True.
    b) False.

4. The basis of dividend growth is

    a) stable and modestly growing profits.

    b) luck.

    c) the competition.

5. Diversification aids stability.

    a) True.

    b) False.

6. Large dividend growth companies have expected five-year earnings per share growth rates of

    a) 4-8 percent a year.

    b) 8-12 percent a year.

    c) 12-16 percent a year.

7. The owners of a publicly traded company are

    a) its lawyers.

    b) the government.

    c) its shareholders.

8. Companies that pay dividends should never buy back shares.

    a) True.

    b) False.

ANSWERS

1. (c)

2. (a)

3. (b)

4. (a)

5. (a)

6. (b)

7. (c)

8. (b)

Whispers

- The vitality of dividends springs from the vigor of fortress-like businesses.

- What is the competition? Ask that first of all of your long-term investments.

- Avoid investing in companies that face rising competition.

- You will do your portfolio an immense amount of good if you invest in companies that face stable or falling competition.

- Stable, modestly growing profits underlies dividend growth.

- Stable companies persist, an essential trait of any investment if you want to be a long-term owner.

- At the dividend growth stage, not only does the company fund itself, but it generates so much extra cash it can afford to pay dividends.

- The following ranges for the earnings per share growth rate – 8-16 percent for a midsize company and 8-12 percent for a large company – ultimately cap the dividend growth rate for dividend growth stocks.

Notes

- Berkshire Hathaway's 1996 Chairman's Letter:

  https://goo.gl/3wrC7K

- Washington Post article on the last Blockbuster in America:

  https://goo.gl/49WiWg

- For more on competition, see Michael E. Porter's *Competitive Strategy.*

- More precisely, market capitalization is share price times number of shares outstanding.

- Conventionally, a value stock is characterized as a stock with, for instance, a low P/E ratio, a high dividend yield, a low price to book ratio, or a low price to cash flow ratio. Typically, no comparison is made to the stock's underlying growth rate. Thus, many financials fall into the value category because P/E ratios are usually low. Likewise, a cyclical stock at the top of the economic cycle falls into the value category because, at the top, earnings are high and P/E ratio is low. Many investors implicitly believe that a value stock signals a bargain. With both these examples, however, the implicit sense that the stock is a bargain, that somehow valuation is favorable and risk is low, is incorrect. With my definition, I do not automatically take a value stock to be a bargain. I merely accept that something has gone wrong.

- Enron: *https://goo.gl/r5q1Lk*

- Kenneth Lay: *https://goo.gl/lOQr9P*

- Jeffrey Skilling: *https://goo.gl/8y8YfL*

- Andrew Fastow: *https://goo.gl/P6JVMI*

- Although shareholders purportedly benefit from dividends and share buybacks, in some ways it does not matter! With dividends, putting aside taxes, when a company pays a dividend the share price falls by the value of the dividend. Likewise, when a company buys back its shares, while earnings per share typically rises, the stock becomes riskier. So, there are offsets. Still, a worse possibility is the company frittering away its cash on silly stuff! For details, see my book, *Investing in Dividend Growth Stocks*.

- *Paying back your shareholders*, a good read from McKinsey, tackling points misunderstood by many authors and investors, including the fact that share buybacks and dividends are essentially the same, share buybacks merely affording companies more flexibility, and how as companies age well-run companies with strong internal returns but modest growth expectations in their markets (our dividend growth companies fit both counts) have no choice but to pay shareholders what they cannot profitably invest: *https://goo.gl/v8fWws*

- *The repurchase revolution, https://goo.gl/eDnvAB*, also a good read, from the *Economist*. ♣

Prelude to Chapter 2

"If a law does not work even in one place where it ought to, it is just wrong."
Richard Feynman

Is coffee good for you? Or bad? Is one alcoholic drink a day good for you? Or bad?

In many areas of study, practitioners do not know which way is up. With so many variables, they get confused. It is no different with investing. With so many variables, investors get confused. They simply do not know which variable is important or even how to prioritize the many variables. You can see this very clearly in the way different experts rank and address the fundamentals of a stock or in the litany of technical indicators that chartists use.

In Chapter 2, we will see that, as a long-term investor, among the literally hundreds of possibilities, there is *one variable, one magic number,* that we simply *must* focus on – yet this number is almost never mentioned on T.V. and it certainly does not take up a prominent spot in stock summaries on leading financial news websites.

This one number informs us about the *quality* of the business (and ultimately, as we shall see in Chapter 3, is intimately related to *your* investment return, *your* most important number). In fact, it is so important, *I impose a minimum requirement of twenty percent for this number for our dividend growth stocks.*

When we pair this twenty percent with stable, moderate underlying market and company growth, almost by magic, the company is able to pay a growing dividend.

To summarize, here is your second dividend growth lesson: **Look for companies with a long-run value of this number, return on beginning equity, of twenty percent or more.**

(If you find the going in the following chapter annoying, or tough, just think of return on beginning equity as a magic number, a magic number signifying an investment return within the company, an investment return *directly* relevant to shareholders. Twenty percent or more, if consistently produced over many years, signifies that the company is a strong business. Done. Remember this and you have appreciated the key fact – and you can skip the nuances in the chapter, and the arithmetic.) ♣

2. Tuesday – The Numbers As Confirmation

"If you have tears prepare to shed them now."
Shakespeare

Too often, almost comically so, it seems, management is overly optimistic. Perhaps it is a matter of survival. Or an excess of little chocolate donuts. Or believing in the future despite the evidence. But history has not always backed management's starry-eyed optimism up.

Never use management's optimism as the sole basis for investing in a company, especially over the long term. What you have to unearth as well are the numerical signposts, the hard numbers that back management's optimism up. It is not that qualitative checks are unimportant. They are: You must check that the company's business is stable and strong, that its future holds ample room for growth, that its management is capable, that the company understands it must pay shareholders their fair share, and that business risks are not excessive. But after you have done your qualitative checks, roll up your sleeves, put on your thinking cap, and take a good hard look at the numbers, the fundamentals. *The numbers must confirm the story.*

PROFITABILITY

"Nothing contributes so much to the prosperity and happiness of a country as high profits." David Ricardo

Be prepared for some accounting talk in this chapter and the next. But do not panic. It is not at all difficult. You only need to understand the *very bare essentials* – you do not need to dive under the hood to understand how the car runs. You simply need to *identify* the keys, the wheels, the brakes, the engine. Grab that cup of coffee on a Tuesday evening. Here we go.

Profitability is the essence of a business. We measure a company's profitability by its **net profit margin** (more simply, profit margin), *earnings divided by sales.* Yahoo! Finance and Value Line publish this ratio. You can also calculate it quite readily. Earnings and sales are part of a company's *income statement* – one of three key financial statements that a company produces at the end of a reporting period.

The purpose of an income statement is to record a company's sales during a period and show how, after deductions, these sales are transformed into earnings, also known as profits. For example, Table 2.1 presents a simplified version of McDonald's 2012 income statement. All numbers are in millions. From the table, McDonald's sales are 27,567. The sum of the next four items – various deductions incurred to make those sales

Sales	**27,567**
Operating costs and expenses	18,962
Interest expense	517
Other expenses	9
Taxes	2,614
Earnings	**5,465**

Table 2.1: McDonald's 2012 income statement, simplified (in millions). Sales minus the sum of the next four items – costs to make those sales and, primarily, payments to debt-holders and the government – equals earnings.

– is 22,102. Earnings are sales minus these deductions. McDonald's 2012 earnings are therefore 27567 - 22102 or 5,465.

For 2012, McDonald's net profit margin, that is earnings divided by sales, is 5465 / 27567 or 20 percent. Incidentally, currently, mid-2018, net profit margins for the typical company range from five percent to eight percent. McDonald's net profit margins are so much higher because of the company's dominant market share and lucrative franchising model.

Do *not* put your long-term investments at risk by investing in companies with weak or varying profits. Stay away from them – or trade them. These companies are often just one downturn or one bad decision away from disaster. *Remember that a long-term investment in a weak company must always end badly. Time hacks away at a weak company's business, slowly but surely sending its share price toward zero.*

By contrast, companies that produce strong and steady profits are ideally suited to long-term investing. Whereas a weak company only gets weaker in time, a strong company only gets stronger.

Always prefer companies with good to strong net profit margins. Currently, mid-2018, a net profit margin of ten to fifteen percent is good. More than fifteen percent is strong.

Current assets	4,922
Other assets	5,787
Net property and equipment	24,677
Assets	**35,386**
Current liabilities	3,403
Long-term debt	13,632
Other	3,057
Debt	**20,092**
Equity	**15,294**

Table 2.2: McDonald's 2012 balance sheet, simplified (in millions).

EFFICIENCY

An idle factory is a waste of company resources – it does the company little good. Indeed, companies generate sales when they put their assets to *productive* use. One way to assess how *effective* they are at doing so is to calculate how much *sales they generate per dollar of assets*, their *efficiency*, here, measured by *sales divided by assets*. Efficiency is not as broadly published as net profit margin. Still, it too is easy to calculate. Sales, as we have seen, are part of the income statement. Assets are part of another financial statement, the *balance sheet*.

A balance sheet is a snapshot of a company's assets, debt, and equity at the end of a reporting period. Think of assets, roughly, as everything with the company's name to it, thus, the buildings that it owns, the equipment that it owns, its financial accounts, and so on. Equity is simply the portion of assets that *shareholders* own. Debt is whatever is left over, that is, the portion of assets that *others* own.

Table 2.2 presents a simplified version of McDonald's 2012 balance sheet. For McDonald's 2012 efficiency, the line that matters is (total) assets, 35,386 (all numbers are in millions). With sales of 27,567, as before, McDonald's 2012 efficiency is 27567 / 35386 or 0.78.

FINANCIAL LEVERAGE

Not quite yin and yang, but, as mentioned, a company's assets are backed by debt and equity. Debt is money lent to the company. Equity is money given to the company in exchange for ownership (shares). Lenders provide debt. Shareholders provide equity. Assets equal debt plus equity.

One way to understand how debt impacts a company's business is to calculate its *financial leverage* (more simply, leverage), *assets divided by equity*. As of mid-2018, Yahoo! Finance and Value Line do not publish this ratio. Still, as with our prior two ratios, it too is easy to calculate. Assets and equity are on a company's balance sheet. Looking at McDonald's again, from Table 2.2, McDonald's assets (all numbers are in millions, no surprises here) are 35,386 with equity of 15,294. Thus, McDonald's 2012 financial leverage is 35386 / 15294 or 2.31.

If a company earns more on the assets financed by its debt than it pays as interest on that debt, shareholders benefit. In addition, because *some* interest expense is tax deductible (it used to be that *all* interest expense was tax-deductible – corporate tax law recently changed), debt is cheaper than it looks. At a tax rate of 25 percent, 6 percent debt costs 4.5 percent. Most companies prefer debt to equity.

The *return-enhancing* value of debt comes at a cost, however. *Debt is risky. If companies cannot pay the interest on their debt when due, or settle, or refinance, they fail.* The broader the sources of debt and the wider the range of maturities, the better. In the second half of 2008, as the capital markets froze, the stock market punished heavily indebted companies that had to refinance. For instance, casino operator Las Vegas Sands fell 94 percent in 2008.

Excess leverage exacts a heavy toll. Often, at precisely the wrong time, it shows its dangerous other side.

Consider Lehman (Figure 2.1). In 2007, Lehman's already high leverage hit 31. With profit margins falling – from 10 percent in 2003 to 7 percent in 2007 – Lehman was cutting a line too fine. Without an adequate cushion, it was asking for trouble if something went wrong. And, in 2008, something did go wrong. As asset prices fell, Lehman

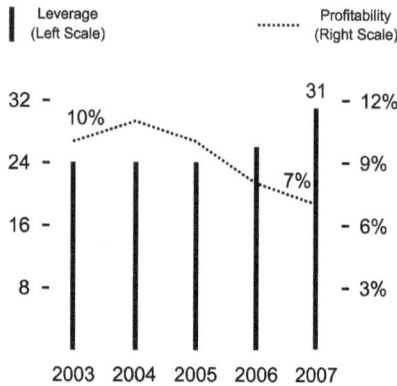

Figure 2.1: Lehman's numbers, trending in the wrong direction and cutting a line too fine.

faced liquidity concerns and a run on the bank. At the same time, its colossal size made it a difficult target for buyers to consider or, perhaps, want to consider. On 15 September 2008, Lehman filed for bankruptcy, in turn, helping precipitate the Crash of 2008.

Prefer companies that use no more than moderate financial leverage. Because companies differ in so many ways, no guideline on financial leverage can universally apply. That said, as a *rough* guideline, *financial leverage less than 2.0 is reasonable.* At 2.0, a dollar of debt is balanced by a dollar of equity. Exceptions abound – though they generally fall into two categories:

- Stable businesses. Companies such as Coca-Cola and IBM carry higher levels of debt because their business stability virtually guarantees that they can pay off their debts when due. How much debt can a stable business handle? It depends on the traits of the business. In general, however, if financial leverage of 2.0 is acceptable for most businesses, financial leverage of (say) 3.0 is acceptable for stable businesses.

- Financial intermediaries. These companies can handle higher levels of debt because all they do is *funnel* money from one part of the economy to another and their businesses are – usually – quite liquid. How much debt can a financial intermediary handle, however, is an open question. For instance, currently, mid-

2018, financial leverage of 15 or more is not uncommon. These companies are different. But as the collapses of Bear Stearns, Washington Mutual, Indy Mac, and Lehman have shown, excess leverage is not without risk.

Financial leverage multiplies a company's return to shareholders. But it cuts both ways. During good times, they benefit. During bad times, they can face ruin. As Warren Buffett has said, "We will reject interesting opportunities rather than over-leverage our balance sheet." Likewise, be wary of companies that use excess financial leverage. In general, avoid them.

ONE NUMBER

Quoting verbatim from *The Aesop for Children*, one of Aesop's Fables, The Monkey and the Dolphin:

> It happened once upon a time that a certain Greek ship bound for Athens was wrecked off the coast close to Piraeus, the port of Athens. Had it not been for the Dolphins, who at that time were very friendly toward mankind and especially toward Athenians, all would have perished. But the Dolphins took the shipwrecked people on their backs and swam with them to shore.
>
> Now it was the custom among the Greeks to take their pet monkeys and dogs with them whenever they went on a voyage. So when one of the Dolphins saw a Monkey struggling in the water, he thought it was a man, and made the Monkey climb up on his back. Then off he swam with him toward the shore.
>
> The Monkey sat up, grave and dignified, on the Dolphin's back.
>
> "You are a citizen of illustrious Athens, are you not?" asked the Dolphin politely.
>
> "Yes," answered the Monkey, proudly. "My family is one of the noblest in the city."
>
> "Indeed," said the Dolphin. "Then of course you often visit Piraeus."

"Yes, yes," replied the Monkey. "Indeed, I do. I am with him constantly. Piraeus is my very best friend."

This answer took the Dolphin by surprise, and, turning his head, he now saw what it was he was carrying. Without more ado, he dived and left the foolish Monkey to take care of himself, while he swam off in search of some human being to save.

Company ABC has high profit margins, moderate efficiency, and high financial leverage. Company XYZ has moderate profit margins, high efficiency, and low financial leverage. Which company is better? Like the Dolphin did with monkey (though inadvertently so), Which one careful question do we ask?

In our case, in general, how do we compare companies when all three numbers matter? One simple, yet highly effective, method is based on the *product* of the three numbers. Instead of comparing three things – and not knowing how to weigh the importance of each – we compare one thing. And the comparison is simple: Higher is better. We call this product, **return on equity**. That is, return on equity is *the product of profit margin, efficiency, and financial leverage*. Using the definitions of these three terms from the three previous sections, return on equity is also, quite simply, *earnings divided by equity*. Continuing with our Happy Meal, with earnings of 5,465 (Table 2.1) and equity of 15,294 (Table 2.2), (yes, as you may have guessed, all numbers are *still* in millions), McDonald's 2012 return on equity is 5465 / 15294 or 36 percent.

It is worth delving into the meaning of this concept more carefully. Earnings are what a company makes ("earns") for its shareholders. Equity is what its shareholders *invest*. Thus, *provided we use equity at the beginning of a year*, return on equity – as a measure of what a company makes for its shareholders divided by what its shareholders invest – is a rough measure of investment return, rough because equity changes during the year but our definition does not reflect these changes. To differentiate this version of the definition from our original one, let us call this version, *return on beginning equity*. For an example, again with McDonald's, see Table 2.3.

Return on beginning equity is an investment return within the company, an internal return. Return on beginning equity is *not* an investment

Return on beginning equity:	
Earnings in 2012	5,465
Equity at the end of the previous year, 2011	14,390
Return on beginning equity [Earnings / Beginning Equity]	**38%**

Table 2.3: McDonald's 2012 return on beginning equity (numbers in millions, except for the calculated value). I consider equity at the beginning of a year the same as equity at the end of the previous year. Thus, McDonald's equity at the beginning of 2012 is the same as McDonald's equity at the end of 2011.

return that you can get as a shareholder. However, and this point is crucial, *the returns are related because internal returns form the basis of shareholder returns.* *Thus, especially for long-term investors, knowing a company's internal return becomes an important part of investing in a company.* *Companies with poor long-term internal returns will never generate good long-term shareholder returns.*

Because we can think of return on beginning equity as a return, we can compare it to other returns. For instance, over a short period, we can compare it to the return on one-year Treasuries. During most years, a company's return on beginning equity should handily beat the return on one-year Treasuries. If not, the company should sell its assets and invest in one-year Treasuries instead. Likewise, shareholders should sell their shares in the company and invest in something else instead – they are not getting adequately compensated for the risk that they are taking.

Always check long-run averages, (say) five- or ten-year averages, of a company's return on equity or return on beginning equity. Long-run averages, like finishing trowels on concrete, smooth out a company's performance. They balance the good years with the bad.

Rising internal returns (with no more than comfortable levels of debt) are good. High and stable internal returns are also good. In general, *avoid making long-term investments in companies with low or unstable or declining internal returns*.

As a guide, *a long-run return on beginning equity average of twenty percent or more is a good internal return.* *We will expect this of our dividend growth stocks.*

Not only is this much higher than typical other returns, but, as we will see in the next chapter, *a twenty percent return on beginning equity allows a company to grow at a sensible and sustainable pace yet pay a reasonable share of its earnings as dividends*. It signals both maturity and high quality.

You may wonder how companies generate such high internal returns. One reason, naturally, is superior business quality. Another reason, perhaps surprisingly, is financial leverage. Financial leverage, *the leverage signifies the effect of a lever*, magnifies internal returns. For many companies, financial leverage holds the key to these high internal returns.

With dividend growth stocks, it gets even better because dividend growth stocks can comfortably take on more financial leverage than an otherwise "equivalent" company without as stable a business. Thus, for dividend growth stocks, internal returns ratchet higher – which eventually translates into higher dividends and higher returns. Still, as always, even for dividend growth stocks, financial leverage should not be taken too far.

A high return – any high return – simply *validates* that the entity is performing well (as long as financial leverage is not too high, the latter implying higher risk). As such, with a *long-run* return on beginning equity average of twenty percent of more, we are simply insisting, *numerically*, that our dividend growth stocks be strong, stable businesses. Simple, right? Yes! But a crucial point sorely missed by many authors and investors!

YOUR TURN

It is worth taking the time to understand the ideas in this chapter well, especially those of profit margin, financial leverage, return on equity, and return on beginning equity. The vocabulary might be onerous if you are not used to it. But the concepts, at the level that we need, and useful for long-term investors, are not that tricky. Some practice with the ideas might help.

Tables 2.4 and 2.5 present simplified versions of Microsoft's 2016 income statement and balance sheet.

Sales	85,320
Operating costs and expenses	65,138
Interest expense	0
Other expenses	431
Taxes	2,953
Earnings	16,798

Table 2.4: Microsoft's 2016 income statement, simplified (in millions).

Current assets	139,660
Other assets	35,678
Net property and equipment	18,356
Assets	193,694
Current liabilities	59,357
Long-term debt	40,783
Other	21,557
Debt	121,697
Equity	71,997

Table 2.5: Microsoft's 2016 balance sheet, simplified (in millions).

Please answer the following questions:

1. Microsoft's profit margin is

   a) 10 percent.

   b) 15 percent.

   c) 20 percent.

2. Microsoft's profit margin is strong.

   a) True.

   b) False.

3. Microsoft's financial leverage is

   a) 2.5.

   b) 2.7.

   c) 2.9.

4. Microsoft's return on equity is

   a) 21 percent.

   b) 22 percent.

   c) 23 percent.

5. If Microsoft's equity at the beginning of the year is 80,083, Microsoft's return on beginning equity is

   a) 21 percent.

   b) 22 percent.

   c) 23 percent.

6. Once you get past the vocabulary, all this jazz is a piece of cake.

   a) True.

   b) False.

Answers:

1. (c)

2. (a)

3. (b)

4. (c)

5. (a)

6. (a)

We have now built up a good portion of our core. In the next chapter, we continue – I tie our friend, dividends, to the man behind the curtain, earnings, establishing many important ideas and relationships along the way. But that's for tomorrow. Take a well-earned break. You deserve it.

Quiz

1. With sales of 100 and earnings of 15, profit margin is

    a) 15 percent.
    b) 100 percent.
    c) 42 percent.

2. Currently, mid-2018, an example of a strong profit margin is

    a) 7 percent.
    b) 12 percent.
    c) 21 percent.

3. Assets equal debt plus equity.

    a) True.
    b) False.

4. With assets of 200 and equity of 100, financial leverage is

    a) 2.
    b) 20.
    c) 200.

5. Return on beginning equity is an internal return.

    a) True.
    b) False.

6. Internal returns form the basis of shareholder returns.

    a) True.
    b) False.

7. A good long-run return on beginning equity average is

    a) 10 percent or less.
    b) 15 percent or less.
    c) 20 percent or more.

8. A twenty percent return on beginning equity allows a company to

a) grow at a comfortable and sustainable pace.

b) pay a reasonable share of its earnings as dividends.

c) do both of the above.

ANSWERS

1. (a)

2. (c)

3. (a)

4. (a)

5. (a)

6. (a)

7. (c)

8. (c)

WHISPERS

- Never use management's optimism as the sole basis for investing in a company, especially over the long term.

- Net profit margin is earnings divided by sales.

- Always prefer companies with good to strong net profit margins. Currently, mid-2018, a net profit margin of ten to fifteen percent is good. More than fifteen percent is strong.

- Efficiency, as defined here, is sales divided by assets.

- Financial leverage is assets divided by equity.

- Excess leverage exacts a heavy toll.

- Return on equity is the product of profit margin, efficiency, and financial leverage. It is also, quite simply, earnings divided by equity.

- Internal returns form the basis of shareholder returns.

- Companies with poor long-term internal returns will never generate good long-term shareholder returns.

- Avoid making long-term investments in companies with low or unstable or declining internal returns.

- A long-run return on beginning equity average of twenty percent or more is a good internal return.

- With a *long-run* return on beginning equity average of twenty percent of more, we are simply insisting, *numerically*, that our dividend growth stocks be strong, stable businesses.

NOTES

- An income statement shows (1) sales; (2) operating costs and expenses incurred to make those sales; (3) interest expense; (4) other expenses; (5) taxes; and (6) earnings. Sales minus the sum of items (2) to (5) equals earnings. Earnings are what shareholders are – theoretically – left with after everyone (and everything) gets their share. These include suppliers, employees, and the accounting costs of things such as land and equipment (combined, these are operating costs and expenses); debt holders (interest expense); and the government (taxes). In addition to earnings, the income statement includes earnings per share.

- More on the interest deduction: *https://goo.gl/Xegm3x*

- The Monkey and the Dolphin: *http://read.gov/aesop/074.html*

- What I call efficiency here – in the name of jargon simplification – is referred to more pedantically, and accurately, as asset turnover ratio. In reality, companies have still other ways of measuring efficiency, though those other ways do not concern us here.

- Some tie the amount of debt that a company can handle to how much it "earns" before adjustments. They use something called EBITDA, that is, earnings before interest, taxes, depreciation, and amortization. I do not take this route.

- Using the definitions of profit margin, efficiency, and financial leverage:

$$Return\ on\ Equity\ =\ \frac{Earnings}{Sales}\ *\ \frac{Sales}{Assets}\ *\ \frac{Assets}{Equity}$$

Striking out the duplicate sales and assets terms, we have the simpler formula for return on equity:

$$Return\ on\ Equity\ =\ \frac{Earnings}{Equity}$$

- I should point out two concerns with return on equity. First, some companies have high returns on equity because they do not need much capital. Examples are consulting firms. These firms depend largely on the knowledge that their consultants bring and not on factories, as an example, and other "hard" assets. There's nothing we can do about this. Just be aware of the possibility. Second, and this is technical, return on equity is upwardly biased because the prices to establish the value of the assets on the balance sheet are many years old. Once again, there is nothing too straightforward we can do about this. In any case, our demand that return on (beginning) equity be high, twenty percent or more, gives us a margin of safety.

- Some investors consider other variables instead of return on beginning equity. For instance, some consider *company-wide* returns – for instance, *return on invested capital.* I prefer looking at returns to equity holders because, as we shall see in Chapter 3, these lead *directly, and simply,* to investor returns. We thus have an *extremely* strong clue that we are on the right track. It is not as if we chose this magic number because it is somehow awesome relative to the hundreds of others one could have picked. Not so. It simply makes sense from 30,000 feet and, as we shall see in the next chapter, from an investor return point of view, mathematically. Mathematics, unlike language and bad reasoning, does not lie. Still, I am mindful of debt. Debt cannot be too large, except in those rare instances when businesses are extraordinarily stable. Others argue that return on equity is not a true return because it is based on accounting values. They use other variations, such as *economic* returns. Although this point is valid, twenty percent – as a relatively high requirement – should be large enough to account for most distortions. In this book, I focus on long-term returns to shareholders. As long as these returns are reasonable, and sustainable, that's good enough for me. ♣

Prelude to Chapter 3

"Do you know the only thing that gives me pleasure? It's to see my dividends coming in." *John D. Rockefeller*

As we've already seen, companies *pay* shareholders directly via dividends or indirectly via share buybacks. With a dividend, shareholders benefit directly, receiving cash. With a share buyback, fewer shares remain, implying remaining shareholders receive a greater piece of the earnings pie – in terms of higher *earnings per share growth*.

In Chapter 3, we will see that *dividend yield and earnings per share growth are two of the three constituents of investor return*. Investor return tells you how well you've done. If you earn 9-10 percent a year, you are doing as well as the stock market over the long term. With our dividend growth stocks, you will often do better. For instance, in 2017, the twenty stocks to consider in my book, *Investing in Dividend Growth Stocks*, returned 23 percent, again beating the market, having done so ten out of the last eleven years, and with less risk than the market, meaning you are more likely to actually *achieve* these returns than with the market or riskier stocks. In 2018, as of 13 September 2018, they are yet again beating the market, up 10.9% for the year, about 0.9 percentage points ahead of the market. Long-term investors in these stocks have benefited handsomely!

For some investors, the primary reason to own dividend-paying stocks, including dividend growth stocks, is income. However, and especially over the long term, dividend growth matters more than initial dividend yield *as long as* dividend growth is large enough, as it is virtually always, almost by definition, for our dividend growth stocks. And what *ultimately* drives dividend growth? As we will see in Chapter 3, earnings per share growth – more than coincidentally, a component of investor return!

To summarize, here is your third dividend growth lesson, really applicable to *any* investment you *ever* make: *Focus on your (investor) return.* ♣

3. Wednesday – Strong Returns

"There's always money in the banana stand."
George Bluth (Arrested Development)

Many of the stocks that participated in the gold rush of the late 1990s NASDAQ rabid bull market (good times!) were young and risky companies that paid little in the way of dividends. As the World Wide Web was nascent, companies *had* to exploit every possible business opportunity, meaning they *had* to invest every possible dollar, meaning, in turn, they simply could *not* have paid out any dividends even if they had somehow wanted to.

With no dividends, everything an investor could hope for was bottled up in the stock price. Initially, stock prices soared. For a while, it looked as if the party would never end. But over-exuberance does eventually end. It runs out of money. It runs out of greed. The party did end. Stock prices collapsed. Investors lost almost everything they had invested. Thanks to leverage, some investors lost even more.

Excess risk feels good on the way up. It is catastrophic on the way down.

How much *should* a company pay out in dividends? It depends. It depends on how successful the company is and where it is in its life cycle:

- A struggling company should pay nothing. It needs all its cash to survive – or try something else.

- A young or vigorously growing company cannot pay anything either, except, perhaps, a token amount. To support its growth it needs cash.

- A mature or slow-growing company can return as much as it wants. It does not need most of its cash because it has little, or nothing, to invest in. (But because it has little, or nothing, to invest in, its growth, if not low already, will eventually slow. Dividend growth will do the same.)

- *Dividend growth companies sit somewhere in the happy middle between young and mature.* They do not grow so quickly that they consume large amounts of cash. They do not grow so slowly that they can return most of their cash to shareholders. What they can do is grow at a reasonable pace *and* pay a reasonable and growing dividend.

DIVIDEND PAYOUT RATIO

"One figure can sometimes add up to a lot." Mae West

"An economist's guess is liable to be as good as anybody else's." Robert Heil-
broner

Dividends are distributions that companies make to their shareholders, typically in cash. Dividends ultimately arise from earnings. The
dividend payout ratio, *dividends per share divided by earnings per share*,
a simple yet important concept, makes this explicit. (If you are not familiar with dividends per share, it is simply (total) dividends divided
by the number of shares outstanding. Similarly, for earnings per share,
(total) earnings divided by the number of shares outstanding.)

I am being slightly cavalier with my definition here. A better definition uses *(total) dividends divided by (total) earnings*, though calculating this is more difficult as total dividends and total earnings are not
as widely distributed as dividends per share and earnings per share.

For example, in the second quarter of 2018, Colgate-Palmolive paid
$0.42 in dividends per share on $0.73 of earnings per share. The company's dividend payout ratio was thus 0.42 / 0.73 or 58 percent.

In this definition, like a shirt with a coordinating tie, dividends per
share and earnings per share must be consistent. Quarterly dividends
per share must pair with quarterly earnings per share. Annual dividends per share must pair with annual earnings per share. And so
on.

To decide how much to pay out as dividends, companies use dividend payout ratio *targets*. Typically, the more mature the company,
the higher the target. *Larger companies typically use dividend payout ratio
targets of 40 percent to 60 percent.*

THE LINK BETWEEN P/E RATIO AND DIVIDEND YIELD

With too many independent ideas, like standing in a spinning room, it
is easy to feel overwhelmed. (After the last chapter, you may already
be there!) In this section, I connect three of our key ideas. These ideas
are not as independent as they seem.

A company's *P/E ratio* is *price per share (P) divided by earnings per share* (E). So a stock with a price of $100 and earnings per share of $5 has a P/E ratio of 100 / 5 or 20. Here, E is an annual value based typically on earnings per share for the trailing four quarters, the next four quarters, or two quarters in the past plus two quarters in the future. On financial websites, P/E ratios based on earnings per share for the trailing four quarters are most common.

Dividend yield is *equivalent annual dividend divided by current stock price. Equivalent annual dividend* is simply the current dividend annualized. Thus, with a quarterly current dividend, it is the quarterly dividend times four. As I write this, mid-2018, IBM trades at $145.16. With a quarterly dividend of $1.57, IBM's equivalent annual dividend is 1.57 * 4 or $6.28. IBM's dividend yield is thus 6.28 / 145.16 or 4.33 percent.

> It is not difficult to show that *P/E ratio equals dividend payout ratio divided by dividend yield.* In other words, *dividend payout ratio provides the link between P/E ratio and dividend yield* – the three ideas are not as independent as they seem.

This result has an important corollary: *Whenever dividend payout ratio is constant (or reasonably so), P/E ratio and dividend yield are opposing faces of the same coin. When one is high, the other must be low.* Thus, for example, when we talk of buying a stock with a high dividend yield we are almost always saying, equivalently, that we are buying a stock with a low P/E ratio. And, assuming the stock pays a dividend, vice versa.

SUSTAINABLE GROWTH RATE

How fast can a company grow without raising net new funds from shareholders? In the Notes section, starting on page 66, at the end of this chapter, I show that, this quantity – called the sustainable growth rate – is given by:

$$Sustainable\ Growth\ Rate$$
$$=\ (1\ -\ Dividend\ Payout\ Ratio)$$
$$*\ Return\ on\ Beginning\ Equity$$

And there's our friend from the previous chapter making its presence known, *return on beginning equity*! As the formula shows, *a company's sustainable growth rate is tied to how much it pays in dividends and the quality of its business.* Pay too much, or run a poor business, and the company's sustainable growth rate suffers.

Knowing a company's long-term sustainable growth rate is crucial to long-term investors because it is the most that a company can grow without raising net new equity. Companies cannot grow slower or faster than this without doing *something* different. If they were growing slower, we would want to know why. If they were growing faster, we would want to know how.

In turn, **long-term sustainable growth rate is linked to growth rate of the company's underlying markets and the company's competitive position within those markets.** Theoretically, companies first judge the growth rates of their markets, then return what they do not need to investors, perhaps keeping a bit for adverse times.

Suppose a company (1) wants to pay half of its earnings as dividends; yet (2) still grow ten percent a year. What should its return on beginning equity be? In the equation above, on substituting a dividend payout ratio of fifty percent and a sustainable growth rate of ten percent, we see that return on beginning equity must equal twenty percent. This result confirms an important observation made in the previous chapter:

A twenty percent return on beginning equity allows a company to grow at a sensible and sustainable pace yet pay a reasonable share of its earnings as dividends. It signals both maturity and high quality.

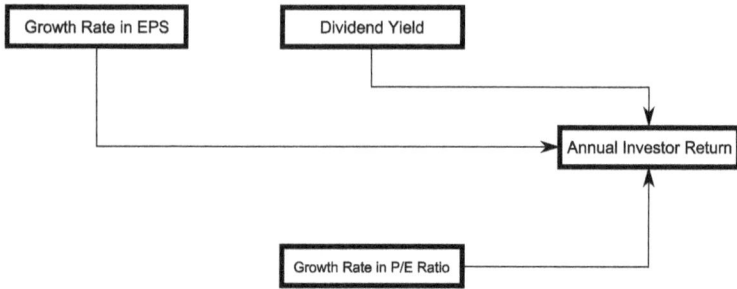

Figure 3.1: Dividend yield, growth rate in earnings per share, and growth rate in P/E ratio as contributors to annual investor return.

INVESTOR RETURN

As a long-term investor, it is important to understand how returns emerge. Without this, it is easy to become distracted, focusing on the wrong things and losing track of what's important.

(When I listen to some professional investors speak, I am not entirely convinced they know of the formula in this section, or at least appreciate its implications! I developed this formula from first principles and (a) algebra and (b) calculus – either way works, the derivation is straightforward. So study it carefully, understand it thoroughly, apply it regularly, and you will be ahead of some professionals and, almost by definition, most non-professionals. It's important.)

What *annual* return can you *expect* from investing in a stock? When you invest in a share of stock, you earn an *annual* return equal to, roughly, the sum of three terms (Figure 3.1):

$$
\begin{aligned}
\textit{Annual Investor Return} \;=\;& \textit{Dividend Yield} \\
+\;& \textit{Growth Rate in Earnings Per Share} \\
+\;& \textit{Growth Rate in P/E Ratio}
\end{aligned}
$$

We know what each term on the right side means. Growth rate, as always, is change (that is, growth) – this period's value minus the prior period's value – divided by the prior period's value.

This formula applies to any stock. As an example, suppose a stock yields 3 percent with expected growth rate in earnings per share of 10 percent. If P/E ratio does not change, we expect the stock to return 3 + 10 percent, or 13 percent. If P/E ratio rises, (say) from 15 to 18, a 20 percent increase, we expect the stock to return 13 + 20 percent, or 33 percent. If P/E ratio falls, (say) from 15 to 12, a 20 percent decrease, we expect the stock to return 13 - 20 percent, or -7 percent.

This last calculation highlights one of the dangers of holding stocks with potentially rapid drops in P/E ratio, a particularly thorny problem when P/E ratio is high: *Even with rapid growth in earnings per share, a big drop in P/E ratio can decimate your returns faster than Carl Icahn can say Gangnam Style.* When you buy a stock with a high P/E ratio, you must be *certain* business momentum can be maintained – or even accelerate.

In our formula, annual return is dividend yield plus something else. We call this something else, the contribution from capital changes. When this contribution is positive, we say we have a *capital gain*. When this contribution is negative, we say we have a *capital loss*. When we hold on to our stock, our gain or loss is *unrealized*. When we sell our stock, our gain or loss is *realized*.

Historically, dividend yield has produced about one-third of market returns; capital gains, about two-thirds. Moreover, of the contribution from capital gains, almost all has come from growth rate in earnings per share. That is, **over long periods, growth rate in P/E ratio has contributed nothing**. Zero. Zilch. Nada. Sometimes, it has added. At other times, it has subtracted. Net, it has produced nothing.

As a broad rule, buy stocks when the market's P/E ratio is reasonable or low. Likewise, buy stable stocks, such as high-quality dividend growth stocks, when their P/E ratios are reasonable or low. A reasonable or low P/E ratio gives you some hope that P/E ratio rises and adds to your returns; or, at least, that P/E ratio does not fall too much and subtract from your returns.

You can generally count on receiving your dividends, especially your dividends from high-quality stocks. Capital gains are another matter. *Capital gains are inherently unstable and fleeting.* A skeptic will say you cannot collect capital gains without the help of a Greater Fool. That is, someone has to step forward and pay more for your shares. Though this notion is widely accepted, it is perhaps a bit untrue. As the formula shows, contribution from capital changes is growth rate in earnings per share plus growth rate in P/E ratio. It seems reasonable that someone will pay for the former because a company typically adds to its value when it grows earnings per share. It is in the latter, however, that the Theory of the Greater Fool has merit. Growth rate in P/E ratio is volatile. It has underpinnings in random things such as psychology and expectations. And random events such as weather and war. It's a bit like throwing a die. Sometimes it comes up six. Sometimes it comes up one. Beforehand, you cannot tell.

FROM RETURN ON BEGINNING EQUITY TO INVESTOR RETURN

> Many investors fixate on dividends. But investor return is the most important thing. After all, a dividend yield of 6 percent does little good if the stock falls 10 percent. What you gain in one pocket, you lose in the other.

Figure 3.2 shows how (annual) investor return develops for dividend growth stocks. *Moreover, it nicely shows the interplay between the three key actors in this drama: company, stock market, and investor,* the stock market acting as *intermediary* between company and investor. Think of company as primarily the boxes in the left column; stock market, the *link* between company and investor, as primarily the boxes in the middle column; and investor, as primarily the boxes in the right column.

In the left column, return on beginning equity is a fundamental company number. It establishes how much the company earns on its shareholders' investment. Dividend payout ratio is a company decision. It is primarily guided by underlying growth rates in the company's business. It equals the portion of earnings that the company can pay out as dividends, yet maintain its growth. What remains of return on beginning equity after paying out dividends translates into growth rate in earnings per share.

In the middle column, P/E ratio is the multiple that the stock market accords the company's earnings per share. Dividend yield is equivalent annual dividend divided by current stock price. Growth rate in P/E ratio contributes to returns but is difficult to forecast.

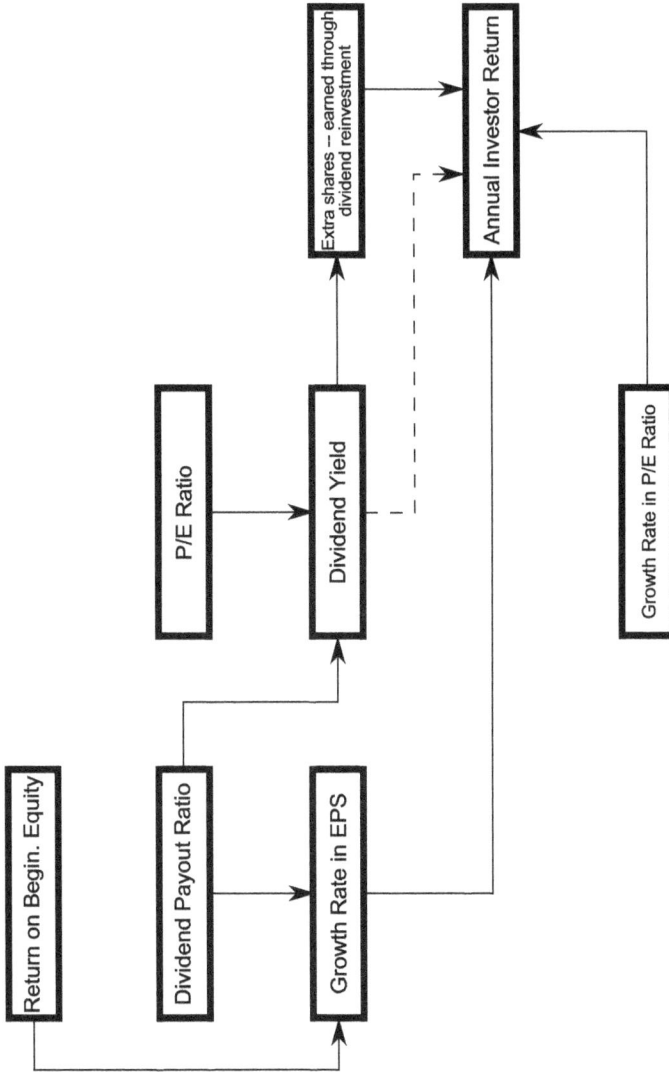

Figure 3.2: How annual investor return develops.

In the right column, the investor has two choices with the dividends that he receives: (1) He may choose to not reinvest his dividends. In this case, dividend yield adds directly to annual investor return. (Moreover, he may earn an extra return on these dividends by investing them in something else.) (2) He may choose to reinvest his dividends. In this case, dividend yield adds indirectly to annual investor return through the extra shares earned through dividend reinvestment. Growth rate in earnings per share and growth rate in P/E ratio also contribute to annual investor return.

(For dividend growth stocks, this completes the picture. With other stocks, another box leads to return on beginning equity. It represents money that the company raises in the stock market. This causes share dilution. It must be incorporated into the calculation of return, normally as a change in growth rate in earnings per share. [For instance, this is especially true with rapidly growing stocks. Because of share dilution, growth rate in earnings per share – thus, ultimately, return as well – is not as high as the investor may have originally believed. Share dilution takes its toll.] Dividend growth stocks are self-funding. They do not need to raise money in the stock market.)

Many investors often make arbitrary estimates of a stock's return. They generate estimates out of thin air. They do not realize the connections among the various pieces. As the figure shows, the various pieces are connected. They lead in a definite path to investor return.

Sip that evening cup of coffee slowly! Read this section several times. Take the time to understand the figure well. Few investors know of this connection, a novel yet simple and important approach to understanding how investor returns develop – and something that you will not find anywhere else. It's very important!

THE PAYOUT RATIO

"By magic numbers and persuasive sound." William Congreve

Except for taxes, share buybacks and dividends are basically the same. (Please see my book, *Investing in Dividend Growth Stocks*, for an argument of why this must be so.) But dividend payout ratio does not account for share buybacks or, for that matter, shares issued. To fix this, we modify it.

Thus, instead of just dividends in the numerator of the dividend payout ratio, we *add cash spent on share buybacks to dividends then subtract cash received from shares issued*. Moreover, some companies behave too conservatively – they keep more cash than they should. *Thus, in addition to these two changes, we also include additional cash that a company can return to shareholders but for whatever reason does not*. We call this new ratio the *payout ratio*. (Do not confuse this terminology with the dividend payout ratio. In this book, I will be careful to mention dividend payout ratio if I am only interested in dividends. The payout ratio is much more important to us.)

The numerator of the payout ratio is the maximum that a company can return to shareholders. Any company can return more than it should, but its growth will then suffer – or it will have to raise money in the markets to compensate. The payout ratio is subjective because we have to estimate the extra part.

All else equal, look for the payout ratio for our dividend growth stocks to average at least fifty percent. This guarantees that companies are paying a reasonable share of their earnings to shareholders and that the companies are suitable candidates – in terms of maturity and quality – for dividend growth investment.

Because payout ratio is the maximum that a company can pay, it removes the discretion of share buybacks. It varies less. Moreover, because of the steady nature of the typical dividend growth company's business, variations are even more muted. Payout ratio thus becomes a "good" ratio – as in calm seas versus choppy seas – for the financial analysis of dividend growth stocks. For us, it plays a prominent role in valuation.

How Companies Grow Their Dividends (per share)

Companies grow their dividends per share through:

- Growth in dividend payout ratio; and

- Growth in earnings per share, which in turn arises from:

  – Growth in earnings; and
  – Reduction in shares outstanding.

(In this section, I emphasize dividends *per share* to carefully differentiate this from (total) dividends. In particular, while in the rest of the book I say dividend growth, in this section, I say dividends per share growth.)

> *The primary factor driving long-term growth rate in dividends per share is growth rate in earnings per share. Earnings per share can keep rising, potentially, forever. Dividend payout ratio cannot. Like arriving at a final destination, it reaches a long-term maximum. This limits its long-term influence.*

But in the short- and intermediate-term, growth in dividend payout ratio can have a dramatic impact on growth in dividends per share. For instance, McDonald's dividends per share rose smartly from $0.215 per share in 2000 to $2.050 per share in 2009. This happened not just because earnings per share rose a robust 12 percent a year – from $1.46 per share in 2000 to $4.11 per share in 2009 – but also because McDonald's dividend payout ratio rose steadily from 15 percent in 2000 to 50 percent in 2009 (Figure 3.3). Investors in McDonald's got a double shot of dividend growth espresso.

This magic cannot continue forever, however – because the dividend payout ratio cannot rise forever. For instance, given its current size, McDonald's dividends per share will never again compound over a reasonably long period, (say) three to five years, at the rate that it did between 2000 and 2009. Like a Michael Jordan dunk, that 28.5 percent compound annual growth rate is history.

Suppose we know, somehow magically, (1) the change in dividend payout ratio from this year to the next; and (2) next year's earnings per share growth rate. Can we calculate *dividends per share growth rate?* Yes. The answer is, roughly, **dividend payout ratio growth rate plus earnings per share growth rate.** As an example, suppose this year's dividend payout ratio is 50 percent, next year's expected dividend payout ratio is 55 percent, and expected earnings per share growth

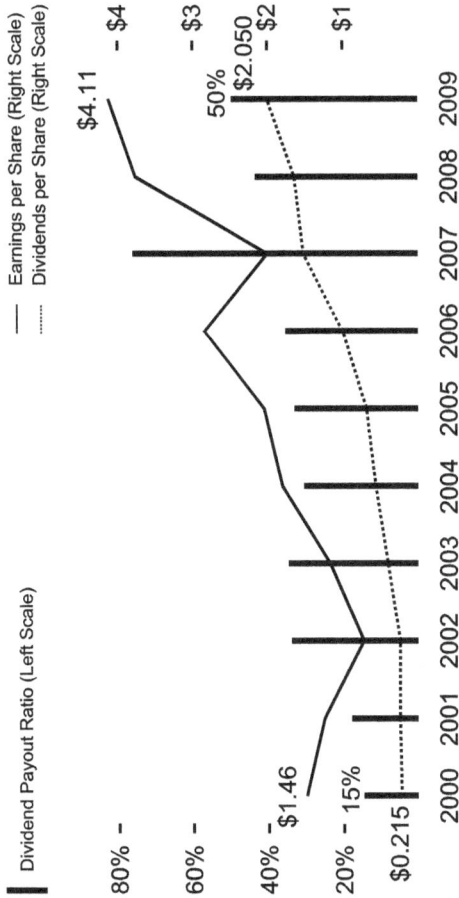

Figure 3.3: McDonald's dividends per share rose smartly from $0.215 per share in 2000 to $2.050 per share in 2009. This happened not just because earnings per share rose a robust 12 percent a year – from $1.46 per share in 2000 to $4.11 per share in 2009 – but also because McDonald's dividend payout ratio rose steadily from 15 percent in 2000 to 50 percent in 2009.

rate is 10 percent. What is the rough expected one-year dividends per share growth rate? The answer is (55 - 50) / 50 + 0.10 or 20 percent.

From this calculation, *once dividend payout ratio does not change, which we typically assume for well-established companies, dividends per share growth rate equals earnings per share growth rate.* In other words, as noted, and this is important, one of those things grossly misunderstood by many authors and many investors and worth reciting five times until it becomes second nature, *earnings per share growth rate is the primary factor driving long-term growth rate in dividends per share.*

All of this is yet another example of where you simply *cannot* take history and blindly extrapolate it. In McDonald's case, it would have been incredibly foolish to extrapolate that 28.5 percent dividends per share growth rate, without realizing that the dividend payout ratio rising was a huge part of the reason for the big increase – and this would simply not repeat. What has happened since 2009? Between 2009 and 2018, McDonald's dividends per share will have risen 8.3 percent a year. Not bad, but, as expected, *nowhere* close to 28.5 percent!

HISTORY

Do not be fooled by small dividend increases. Long-term dividend increases must average far more than inflation. Otherwise, you are losing out. You are not getting paid for the risk that you are taking. Be wary of companies that raise their dividends by the tiniest of amounts.

Use the following resources to research a company's dividend history:

- **Company investor relations websites**.

- **Value Line's** *Investment Survey*, available at most libraries, if not as a printed copy, then at least online.

- As of mid-2018, **Yahoo! Finance** includes dividend history on each stock's *Historical Data* page.

Do not feel compelled to research a company's *entire* dividend history. Ten to fifteen years is ample – dividends paid during Nixon's presidency do us little good. Ultimately, we want to know what the *future* will bring. We are *far* less interested in the distant past. Check that the company's dividend growth rate has exceeded long-term inflation, three percent. Always watch for problems such as decreases. Check the trend. If the trend has changed, ask why. Was it because of the economy? Or was it because of something company-specific or industry-related? Does the change look temporary? Or permanent?

In addition to dividend history, research the history of the dividend payout ratio. Value Line has a ten-year history of the dividend payout ratio. As before, study the trend. Is it stable, increasing, or decreasing? Stability does not mean dividend payout ratio has to be constant. It just means that it is reasonably bounded, for instance, between 45 percent and 50 percent, with no obvious trend. Earnings sometimes dip for onetime reasons. This disrupts the trend.

Do not discard a stock simply because of a limited or damaged dividend history. With a limited history, you can view the start of a dividend as a sign of confidence, or maturity, or both. Likewise, a damaged dividend history is not necessarily the end of the world. Even big companies make mistakes serious enough that they have to lower their dividends. If they resume their dividends, however, take another look. For instance, in the early 2000s, Lockheed Martin slashed its dividend to pay down debt. Since then, it has emerged stronger. It has bought back shares. It has raised its dividend.

Conversely, a strong dividend history does not always suggest a strong dividend growth stock. The past does not necessarily extrapolate without error. Pay attention to dividend history but do not be fooled by it. *The 800-pound gorilla in the room is how the business performs in the future.* Consider Lehman. Between 2002 and 2006, the company grew its dividend at a more than 25 percent a year clip. Lehman outperformed the market and many of its peers. Yet, in 2008, in the blink of an investment eye, the company declared bankruptcy. The dividend was gone. Lehman's dividend history proved meaningless.

For now, the hard work is done! Thursday will be a much easier day. In the next chapter, we learn how to select our favorite long-term stocks.

QUIZ

    1. Dividend payout ratio is dividends per share divided by

    a) stock price.

    b) total earnings.

    c) earnings per share.

2. P/E ratio equals dividend payout ratio divided by dividend yield.

    a) True.

    b) False.

3. If return on beginning equity is 20 percent and dividend payout ratio is 60 percent, sustainable growth rate is

    a) 48 percent.

    b) 8 percent.

    c) 12 percent.

4. To long-term investors, knowing the long-term sustainable growth rate is

    a) unimportant.

    b) optional.

    c) crucial.

5. Over the long term, growth rate in P/E ratio has contributed nothing to investor return.

    a) True.

    b) False.

6. For us, payout ratio is much more important than dividend payout ratio.

    a) True.

    b) False.

7. The primary factor driving the long-term dividends per share growth rate is

    a) growth rate in dividend payout ratio.

    b) growth rate in earnings per share.

    c) growth rate in employee count.

8. Dividend payout ratio cannot keep rising forever.

    a) True.

    b) False.

ANSWERS

1. (c)

2. (a)

3. (b)

4. (c)

5. (a)

6. (a)

7. (b)

8. (a)

WHISPERS

- Dividends are distributions that companies make to their shareholders, typically in cash.

- Dividend payout ratio is dividends per share divided by earnings per share. A better definition uses (total) dividends divided by (total) earnings.

- Dividend yield is equivalent annual dividend divided by current stock price.

- P/E ratio is price divided by earnings per share. It is also dividend payout ratio divided by dividend yield.

- Whenever dividend payout ratio is constant (or reasonably so), P/E ratio and dividend yield are opposing faces of the same coin. When one is high, the other must be low.

- Knowing a company's long-term sustainable growth rate is crucial to long-term investors because it is the most that a company can grow without raising net new equity.

- Long-term sustainable growth rate is linked to growth rate of the company's underlying markets and the company's competitive position within those markets.

- A twenty percent return on beginning equity allows a company to grow at a sensible and sustainable pace yet pay a reasonable share of its earnings as dividends.

- For any stock, annual investor return is, roughly, dividend yield plus growth rate in earnings per share plus growth rate in P/E ratio.

- Over long periods, growth rate in P/E ratio has contributed nothing to annual investor return.

- For us, payout ratio is crucial. It is more important than dividend payout ratio.

- All else equal, look for the payout ratio for our dividend growth stocks to average at least fifty percent.

- The primary factor driving long-term growth rate in dividends per share is growth rate in earnings per share.

- Pay attention to dividend history but do not be fooled by it. The 800-pound gorilla in the room is how the business performs in the future.

Notes

- Though we often use loose language to imply otherwise, dividends are not paid out of earnings. Dividends are paid out of cash. In theory, therefore, and contrary to what the dividend payout ratio implies, we must exercise care comparing dividends and earnings. Instead, we must compare like with like. We must compare dividends with cash-based metrics. As a side benefit, when we use cash-based metrics, we quickly discover whether a company can *afford* to pay its dividends. Typical cash-based metrics are various forms of a company's cash flow.

- If dividends are paid out of cash, why then do so many investors look at the dividend payout ratio? Because cash flow is volatile. Earnings are much less so – as a side benefit of accounting rules. As a result, dividend to cash flow ratios behave like a bouncing ball – whereas dividend payout ratio is comparatively stable. Moreover, over a company's lifetime, total earnings equal total free cash flow. In a cumulative sense, therefore, we are looking at the same thing. Investors typically look at dividend to

cash flow ratios for companies in distress. In such cases, understanding whether a company can continue to pay its dividend
becomes paramount. Comparing dividends to cash flow for our
– typically strong – dividend growth companies does not get you
much.

- With P as price per share, E as earnings per share, and D as dividends per share, the following equation holds as the P's cancel:

$$\frac{P}{E} * \frac{D}{P} = \frac{D}{E}$$

Dividing both sides by $\frac{D}{P}$:

$$\frac{P}{E} = \frac{\left(\frac{D}{E}\right)}{\left(\frac{D}{P}\right)}$$

In English:

$$P/E \ Ratio = \frac{Dividend \ Payout \ Ratio}{Dividend \ Yield}$$

- If a portfolio experiences no deposits and no withdrawals in a
given year, *the portfolio's growth rate* – its change in equity (equity is what the portfolio holder owns) divided by its equity at
the beginning of the year – matches its rate of return. It has
to. The money could not have come from anywhere else. For
companies, the logic is identical, except that dividends weave
in a little wrinkle. Dividends are akin to withdrawals. Without
dividends, a company's growth equals its earnings. Dividends
reduce a company's growth by exactly the amount of the dividends. Thus, *growth = earnings - dividends*. Importantly, as with
the portfolio, *this relationship assumes no net "deposits," that is, no
net additions to a company's equity.* We call this amount of growth,
sustainable growth. Thus, more accurately:

$$\textit{Sustainable Growth}$$
$$= \;(\textit{Earnings} \;-\; \textit{Dividends})$$

Factoring earnings out of the piece in parentheses and using dividend payout ratio as dividends divided by earnings:

$$\textit{Sustainable Growth}$$
$$= \;(1 \;-\; \textit{Dividend Payout Ratio}) \;*\; \textit{Earnings}$$

Dividing both sides by *beginning equity* and using return on beginning equity as earnings divided by beginning equity:

$$\textit{Sustainable Growth Rate}$$
$$= \;(1 \;-\; \textit{Dividend Payout Ratio})$$
$$* \;\textit{Return on Beginning Equity}$$

- Taxes and annual investor return: *With taxes,* **after-tax** *return is* **after-tax** *dividend yield plus growth rate in earnings per share and growth rate in P/E ratio.* Dividends are taxed. The other two terms are not. This assumes you hold on to your stock. By contrast, if you sell, there are two cases. (1) If you sell with a capital gain, you pay taxes on the capital gain. (2) If you sell with a capital loss, you are (naturally) not taxed on the loss. In fact, you can use the loss to offset certain other taxes, thus reducing your total tax. In effect, the government subsidizes part of the loss, Uncle Sam sharing in the pain.

- The exact expression for dividends per share growth rate in terms of dividend payout ratio, DPR, and earnings per share growth rate, EPSGR, is more complex:

$$\left(1 \;+\; \frac{DPR_{next\,year} \;-\; DPR_{this\,year}}{DPR_{this\,year}}\right) \;*\; (1 \;+\; EPSGR) \;-\; 1$$

This expression is unwieldy. Our approximation usually suffices. ♣

Prelude to Chapter 4

"Success is a lousy teacher. It seduces smart people into thinking they can't lose."

Bill Gates

The requirements that we impose on our dividend growth stocks – qualitatively (stable or falling competition, among others), quantitatively (long-run return on beginning equity of twenty percent or more, among others) – are demanding. *Very few stocks make the cut.*

However, we still need a way to find these very few – otherwise this book is a waste of my time and your time and your money. In Chapter 4, I present two ways, one easy, a piece of cake really, and one requiring more work, a bit more painful.

The easy way is a shameless application of the dictum, "imitation is the sincerest form of flattery." Here, we simply peek at the holdings of well-run dividend growth funds. I list tables of stocks uncovered this way, including two that use a neat shortcut to reduce the selections to a manageable few. You will find these tables useful.

The more painful way involves screening. Unlike what you may have heard, screening is *not* a panacea. With screening, it is *very* easy to overlook good prospects – perhaps because the data have errors or the criteria are too rigid.

Nevertheless, screening can help establish a starting point. In the following chapter, I provide a link to an already populated dividend growth screen, allowing you to instantly give dividend growth screening a whirl.

To summarize, lesson 4 is not really a lesson – it's just an affirmation of our earlier theory: ***Yes, Virginia, dividend growth stocks are a select group.*** ♣

4. Thursday – Prospecting For Stalwarts

"Ponder and deliberate before you make a move."
Sun-tzu

With the information spigot never really turned off these days, you'd expect the search for dividend growth stocks to be easy. It isn't. As with an excess of anything, much of the trumpeted value is noise. Almost everyone focuses on the short term. As a long-term investor, you will find little of value here.

The pundits muse: What will Intel's earnings per share be tomorrow? Why did so-and-so cut Intel's earnings per share estimate one cent? Unless Intel is egregiously overvalued or the questions have longer-term implications, the value of questions such as these to long-term investors is nil. Business fluctuates. For a good company, most fluctuations are blips. More relevant: What can Intel do to offset the decline in its PC business? How will Intel address new markets? What is Intel's long-term growth rate? These questions have a bearing on Intel's long-term return. What Intel earns tomorrow rarely does.

So, when prospecting for your long-term investment ideas, read, watch, and listen – but focus on those who ask the right questions. Prefer long-term insight and careful analysis. Tune out the noise.

Holdings of Mutual Funds, ETFs, and Indexes

"The majority of those who put together collections of verses or epigrams resemble those who eat cherries or oysters; they begin by choosing the best and end by eating everything." Chamfort

Holdings of mutual funds and ETFs (exchange-traded funds) afford us a wealth of investment ideas. The experts do some of the hard work for us. We then winnow down their selections to a manageable few. (Of course, if we like enough of their selections – and do not mind the expenses – we can choose to simply buy the mutual fund or ETF.)

Two caveats:

- Only consider funds with good long-term records.

- Only consider funds with low turnover. Low turnover is twenty percent or less. With high turnover, what is a brilliant new idea one month somehow becomes a pariah the next, the stock quickly going from hero to villain, from Batman to the Joker, not quite the *long*-term story that we are looking for!

Microsoft
Johnson & Johnson
Walmart
PepsiCo
3M
McDonald's
Medtronic
Union Pacific
Abbott
Texas Instruments

Table 4.1: Top ten stocks in VDAIX as of 31 July 2018.

One good source of dividend growth investment ideas is Vanguard's Dividend Appreciation Index Fund Investor Shares, VDAIX, a mutual fund – or Vanguard Dividend Appreciation ETF, VIG, its ETF clone. In its May 2018 prospectus, Vanguard describes VDAIX's investment approach as follows:

> The Fund employs an indexing investment approach designed to track the performance of the NASDAQ US Dividend Achievers Select Index, which consists of common stocks of companies that have a record of increasing dividends over time. The Fund attempts to replicate the target index by investing all, or substantially all, of its assets in the stocks that make up the Index, holding each stock in approximately the same proportion as its weighting in the Index.

In Table 4.1, I list the top ten stocks in VDAIX as of 31 July 2018.

Another good source is Franklin Rising Dividends Fund (Class A Shares), FRDPX. Although this fund has a front-end load and a 12b-1 charge, turnover is extremely low and it has fared well. In its February 2018 prospectus, Franklin Templeton, the fund's parent, describes FRDPX's investment approach as follows:

> Under normal market conditions, the Fund invests at least 80% of its net assets in investments of companies that have

Microsoft
Roper
Becton Dickinson
Honeywell
Stryker
Praxair
Albemarle
Accenture
Texas Instruments
Medtronic

Table 4.2: Top ten stocks in FRDPX as of 31 July 2018.

paid consistently rising dividends. The Fund invests pre-
dominantly in equity securities, primarily common stock.
Companies that have paid consistently rising dividends
include those companies that currently pay dividends on
their common stocks and have maintained or increased
their dividend rate during the last four consecutive years.

In Table 4.2, I list the top ten stocks in FRDPX as of 31 July 2018.

Moving to indexes, the S&P 500® Dividend Aristocrats® index and
the NASDAQ US Dividend Achievers™ Select Index – mentioned by
Vanguard above – offer a rich vein of dividend growth investment
ideas. In Table 4.3, I list the top ten S&P 500 Dividend Aristocrats as
of 31 August 2018. Similarly, in Table 4.4, I list the top ten stocks in
the NASDAQ US Dividend Achievers Select Index as of 29 June 2018,
not surprisingly, even though the dates differ, and the ranking differs,
identical in composition to those of Table 4.1.

Always consider stocks common to high-quality investment vehicles, for us, (say) a VDAIX and an FRDPX. Although this method
favors large-caps, when a stock is present in more than one vehicle
it means it has passed more than one battery of tests. Success, like
thanksgiving turkey, likes company. In Table 4.5, I list the stocks common to VDAIX and FRDPX as of 31 July 2018.

If you find this list too long, as I do, you can continue the process. For instance, in Table 4.6, I list the stocks common to VDAIX,
FRDPX, and another dividend growth fund, the T. Rowe Price Dividend Growth Fund, PRDGX. In this table, the stocks for VDAIX and

Clorox
Emerson Electric
Target
Walmart
Kimberly-Clark
Lowe's
Medtronic
Dover
Cincinnati Financial
Air Products and Chemicals

Table 4.3: Top ten S&P 500 Dividend Aristocrats stocks as of 31 August 2018.

Microsoft
Walmart
Johnson & Johnson
PepsiCo
McDonald's
3M
Medtronic
Union Pacific
Texas Instruments
Abbott

Table 4.4: Top ten stocks in the NASDAQ US Dividend Achievers Select Index as of 29 June 2018.

FRDPX are as of 31 July 2018. Unfortunately, at the time of analysis, the only data available for PRDGX was as of 30 June 2018. Though not ideal – as the dates should match – because PRDGX generally does not have high turnover (its May 2018 prospectus indicates 16 percent turnover, a bit higher than it has been recently, though still not excessive) this anomaly should not pose too much of a problem.

Looking over this table *very* quickly, these stocks would make an *excellent* long-term portfolio for most investors.

Abbott	Johnson & Johnson
ABM Industries	Matthews
Accenture	McCormick
Aflac	McDonald's
Air Products and Chemicals	Medtronic
Albemarle	Microsoft
Analog Devices	Nike
Becton Dickinson	Nucor
Bunge	PepsiCo
Carlisle	Perrigo
Cintas	Roper
Colgate-Palmolive	Ross Stores
CVS Health	Stanley Black & Decker
Donaldson Company	Stryker
Dover	Texas Instruments
Ecolab	Tiffany
Erie Indemnity	United Technologies
General Dynamics	Walmart
Grainger (W. W.)	Walgreens Boots Alliance
John Wiley & Sons	West Pharmaceutical Services

Table 4.5: Stocks common to VDAIX and FRDPX as of 31 July 2018.

Accenture	Microsoft
Air Products and Chemicals	Nike
Becton Dickinson	PepsiCo
Colgate-Palmolive	Roper
CVS Health	Ross Stores
Ecolab	Stanley Black & Decker
Johnson & Johnson	Stryker
McCormick	Texas Instruments
McDonald's	United Technologies
Medtronic	

Table 4.6: Stocks common to VDAIX, FRDPX, and PRDGX.

> Dividend growth stocks are a select group. There simply aren't that many around. Tables such as these are useful.

Screens

"I knew I should've checked your showboating Globetrotter algebra." Professor Farnsworth (Futurama)

If you are willing to put in the effort, screening is another way to find dividend growth stocks. But don't get too excited. You will often overlook good prospects. Screeners often have gaping holes in them. They are not foolproof. They are not thorough. The data have errors. Still, they can help establish a starting point.

First, a few general comments about stock screeners:

- Consider using more than one stock screener. See which stocks overlap across the stock screeners that you use.

- Only screen with mutually exclusive screening variables.

- Ideally, restrict screening variables to just a few, (say) 4 to 6. In any case, try not to exceed 10.

- Look at the stock screener's preset screens. See if they are useful as is. Or if they can be easily modified.

- Look at the results from stock screeners in popular financial magazines and websites.

- Some variables – profit margin, for instance – are point-in-time values. But if an investment is held long term, longer-term averages are better.

- What if you get too many results? It can be hair-pulling and time-consuming to comb through long lists of stocks.

- Stock screening is a first step. Do not quibble over minor details.

In a perfect world for dividend growth stocks, stock screeners would have the following screening variables:

- Quality

  - Return on Beginning Equity (most recent year, or, ideally, a longer-term average, such as a five- or ten-year average)
  - Return on Equity (most recent year, or, ideally, a longer-term average, such as a five- or ten-year average)

- Shareholder Commitment

  - Dividend Payout Ratio, or, even better, some variation of our Payout Ratio.

- Return

  - Expected EPS Growth Rate (current, or, ideally, a five-year average)
  - Historical EPS Growth Rate (a longer-term average, such as a five- or ten-year average)

- Risk

  - Financial Leverage
  - Market Capitalization
  - Beta

You may wonder why I do not include quasi-valuation point-in-time variables such as P/E ratio and dividend yield as screening variables here. Personally, I prefer to separate screening from valuation. That way, if I like a business but the stock is expensive, I have at least found a good company. I can keep an eye on it. You may disagree with my approach. If so, include P/E ratio and dividend yield in your screens. Because dividend payout ratio, P/E ratio, and dividend yield are related, you do not need to include all three in your screen. Any two will do.

I covered these variables before, except for beta. Beta is a variable from Modern Portfolio Theory. It has multiple interpretations. For us, it gauges risk relative to the market by how much the stock moves relative to the market. A stock's beta can be negative, zero, or positive. Most stocks have positive betas. A beta of 0.6 means the stock has historically moved, and, by extension, is expected to move 60 percent of what the market moves. For instance, if the market moves 10 percent, the stock has historically moved, and is expected to move, 6 percent. In this sense, beta measures a stock's "springiness." The market has a beta of 1.0. Most large-cap dividend growth stocks have betas between 0.5 and 0.8, give or take 0.1. These reflect their superior business stability – thus lower risk – relative to the market. Do not treat these values as sacrosanct – betas do change. In recent years, beta has come under attack. Many think, as I do, that it is simplistic.

I use market capitalization as an indicator of risk because, all else equal, the larger the stock the lower the risk. If your screener does not have dividend payout ratio, you will need to include dividend yield as a screening variable, if for no other reason than to get stocks that pay dividends.

Consider including additional *descriptive* variables in your screen. For instance, you may want to exclude non-U.S. stocks, REITs, and MLPs. You may also want to restrict your selections to stocks with share prices above a minimum price, (say) $25. Do not add variables that overlap existing variables. Likewise, do not add so many variables that the screen results in few or no stocks. A good guideline is to have at most ten variables. Start with the ones here, then add yours.

In our list, some variables are preferred. Others are alternatives. Use an alternative if the screener does not have the preferred variable. See Table 4.7. From the table, enter one variable each from categories 1-6. Within each category, when multiple options are available, A is best, B is second, C is third, and D is fourth. If the screener has A, use it. If A is unavailable, use B, and so on. If using all categories results in too few stocks, remove the variables in reverse categorical order. That is, remove category 6 first and see if you get enough stocks. If not, remove category 5, and so on. Do not remove more than three categories. Instead, relax the criteria. For the longer-term averages, a ten-year average is ideal followed by a five-year average. In the table, I use 2.0 Billion to select midcaps and larger, appropriate as of mid-2018. In later years, you will need to adjust this value as ranges of market capitalization bubble up over time. The criteria are generous by design so as not to overlook good prospects. (For instance, if we use a stricter dividend payout ratio criterion of at least forty percent, we will potentially miss companies with lower dividend payout ratios but aggressive share buybacks. Our criteria can *never* be perfect. For instance, with our current dividend payout ratio criterion of at least twenty percent, we will miss companies with dividend payout ratios of nineteen percent and aggressive share buybacks.) Tighten them if you get too many results. A well-designed screen in a normal market

Variables	Categories - Preferences	Criteria
Quality: Return on Beginning Equity		
Most Recent Year	(1 - C)	>= 20%
Longer-Term Average	(1 - A)	>= 20%
Quality: Return on Equity		
Most Recent Year	(1 - D)	>= 20%
Longer-Term Average	(1 - B)	>= 20%
Shareholder Commitment:		
Dividend Payout Ratio	(2 - B)	>= 20%
Payout Ratio (some variant)	(2 - A)	>= 40%
Return: EPS Growth Rate		
Expected, Current	(3 - C)	>= 8%
Expected, Five-Year Average	(3 - A)	>= 8%
Historical, Longer-Term Average	(3 - B)	>= 8%
Risk:		
Financial Leverage	(4)	<= 3.0
Market Capitalization	(5)	>= 2.0 Billion
Beta	(6)	<= 0.9, positive

Table 4.7: Dividend growth screening variables, categories - preferences, and criteria. In general, return on equity does not equal return on beginning equity. Thus, strictly speaking, criteria for return on equity should differ from criteria for return on beginning equity. But for a screen, this difference is not crucial.

should result in (say) thirty to sixty stocks as initial dividend growth candidates – if so, the porridge is probably just right. If you get hundreds, the porridge is too hot, scalding even. If you get ten, that too is (usually) a problem – the porridge is too cold.

Of the free stock screeners available on the web as of mid-2018, Finviz is the best. It is easy to use and offers most of the variables we need (Table 4.8). The free version of Finviz is unusual. It offers only *predefined ranges*, meaning, you cannot enter the exact values of Table 4.7. Instead, you have to choose a suitable range. Sometimes this may not be enough because the ranges we need are not available. Just choose a more generous range. Then sort your results to narrow your choices further. For instance, the Finviz variable "EPS growth next 5 years" includes ranges of "over 5 percent" and "over 10 percent." We cannot enter our criterion of at least 8 percent. To overcome this restriction, choose "over 5 percent" and sort your results by "EPS growth next 5 years." You will now see the subset of results with growth rates of at least 8 percent. Ignore the rest. Finviz does not use financial leverage, as such. It uses a related variable, total debt divided by equity, instead. Finviz calls this Debt/Equity. Because our financial leverage equals total debt divided by equity plus 1, our financial leverage criterion of <= 3.0 becomes <= 2.0, when applied to total debt divided by equity. For us, Finviz's useful options here are "Under 1" and "Over 1." "Under 2" is unavailable. The screen has to be run twice, once with "Under 1" and once with "Over 1" and analyzed. Because of this complication, I just skip Debt/Equity with Finviz. I worry about it later in the selection process.

You can access the Finviz stock screener at the following web address:

- Finviz: *https://goo.gl/c9UnZ*

I populated a dividend growth screen in Finviz here:

- Finviz dividend growth screen: *https://goo.gl/qZVOUM*

For this screen, I used the following variables and criteria:

- Market Cap. +Mid (over $2bln).

- Beta. Under 1.

- EPS growth next 5 years. Over 5%.

- Payout Ratio (this is dividend payout ratio, not payout ratio as I have defined it in this book). Over 20%.

- Return on Equity. Over +20%.

Variables	Availability on Finviz
Quality: Return on Beginning Equity	
Most Recent Year	no
Longer-Term Average	no
Quality: Return on Equity:	
Most Recent Year	yes
	(last 12 months)
Longer-Term Average	no
Shareholder Commitment:	
Dividend Payout Ratio	yes
Payout Ratio (some variant)	no
Return: EPS Growth Rate	
Expected, Current	yes
Expected, Five-Year Average	yes
Historical, Longer-Term Average	yes
	(5-year)
Risk:	
Financial Leverage[*]	yes
Market Capitalization	yes
Beta	yes

Table 4.8: Availability of variables for the Finviz stock screener, as of mid-2018. [*]Not financial leverage as such, but a related variable, total debt divided by equity, instead.

I skipped Debt/Equity. Beta is slightly generous. "EPS growth next 5 years" is generous, as mentioned above. When I ran this screen in mid-2018, I got 98 candidates.

Value Line, which you should be able to access through your local library, has a good stock screener. Value Line's data is likely much better than average because the data has likely been "scrubbed." In general, you will probably get fewer results with Value Line's screener because Value Line follows a smaller universe of stocks. For us, this should not matter. Our dividend growth stocks are well-established companies. Most are likely already included in Value Line's universe.

Use the following Value Line variables and criteria:

- Quality

    - % Return on Shareholder's (sic) Equity (under Valuation Ratios), 3-5 years out (select in a drop-down). Set 20 percent as the minimum.

- To get stocks that pay dividends

    - Include Divided Yield (under Valuation Ratios). Set the minimum to be *greater* than 0 percent. So something like 0.01 percent.

- Return

    - Proj 3-5 Yr EPS Growth Rate (under Projections). Set 8 percent as the minimum.

- Risk

    - Market Cap (under Company Data). Set 2000 (in millions) as the minimum.

    - Financial Strength (under Ranks & Ratings). Select A++, A+, A.

    - Beta (under Company Data). Set 0 as the minimum and 0.9 as the maximum.

When I ran this screen in mid-2018, I got 28 candidates, my kind of number!

Value Line's *Investment Survey* also regularly screens for dividend growth stocks. Other publications may do the same. Understand the criteria that Value Line and these other publications use.

Finally, among other well-known stock screeners, you may want to consider the Zacks stock screener. You can access the screener at the following web address:

- Zacks: *https://goo.gl/9gr676*

Many investors fail to value their stocks or, worse, value them incorrectly. In the next chapter, I turn to the crucial concept of valuation, a concept that is almost *never* covered correctly – thus perpetuating the roller-coaster ride of bad results – and present an original yet easy to use valuation methodology to value our dividend growth stocks.

QUIZ

1. Tune out the market noise because

    a) it focuses on the short term.

    b) it generally lacks long-term insight.

    c) of both of the above.

2. Low turnover for a fund is

    a) 40 percent to 60 percent.

    b) 20 percent or less.

    c) 60 percent to 80 percent.

3. Always consider stocks common to high-quality investment vehicles because

    a) such stocks have passed more than one battery of tests.

    b) larger stocks are always better than smaller stocks.

    c) misery likes company.

4. Checking the holdings of funds is more productive than screening.

    a) True.

    b) False.

5. Variables in screens must be mutually exclusive.

    a) True.

    b) False.

6. Beta is

a) the fourth letter of the Greek alphabet.

b) a gauge of a stock's risk relative to the market.

c) a sound a duck makes.

Answers

1. (c)

2. (b)

3. (a)

4. (a)

5. (a)

6. (b)

Whispers

- Fund holdings afford us a wealth of investment ideas.

- VDAIX – or its ETF clone, VIG – is an excellent source of investment ideas. So is FRDPX.

- Always consider stocks common to high-quality investment vehicles, for us, (say) a VDAIX and an FRDPX. If you get too many results, throw in another dividend growth fund, (say) PRDGX.

- Finviz provides a capable free stock screener. Value Line also has a good stock screener.

Notes

- VDAIX: *https://goo.gl/jvElCl*

- VIG: *https://goo.gl/nkvKB8*

- FRDPX: *https://goo.gl/XmZARQ*

- From its prospectus, more on the investment strategy that FRDPX espouses. This investment strategy is a good example of the kind of approach that an investor should take – though I could quibble with a few points – in terms of getting to the primary points and being thorough. (A) relates to company consistency and maturity. (B) ensures that the dividend growth rate is reasonable. (C) implies that the company is a true dividend *growth* company, that is, it still has areas to invest. (D) suggests reasonable financial risk. (E) reflects (relative) valuation. Quoting from its February 2018 prospectus (I introduce the letters, A to E):

  Under normal market conditions, the Fund invests at least 65% of its net assets in securities of companies that have: (A) consistently increased dividends in at least 8 out of the last 10 years and have not decreased dividends during that time; (B) increased dividends substantially (at least 100%) over the last 10 years; (C) reinvested earnings, paying out less than 65% of current earnings in dividends (except for utility companies); (D) either long-term debt that is no more than 50% of total capitalization (except for utility companies) or senior debt that has been rated investment grade by at least one of the major bond rating organizations; and (E) attractive prices, either: (1) in the lower half of the stock's price/earnings ratio range for the past 10 years; or (2) less than the price/earnings ratio of the Standard & Poor's® 500 Stock Index (this criterion applies only at the time of purchase).

- PRDGX: *https://goo.gl/FtZI7r*

- S&P 500® Dividend Aristocrats® index: *https://goo.gl/GzujEl*

- NASDAQ US Dividend Achievers™ Select Index:

  https://goo.gl/Ka67fs

- A criticism of beta: *https://goo.gl/1wZoVs* ♣

Prelude to Chapter 5

"Everything should be made as simple as possi-
ble, but not simpler."   *Albert Einstein*

You will often read that a stock is cheap because relative to this or that it is cheaper. Or some will say, look at the stock's dividend yield, you are being paid to wait! Or look at the chart! No, no, no.

As a long-term investor – after you have checked that a stock passes the other requirements in this book – you have one final question: "What is the stock's long-term expected return (taking into account risk)?"

Yet, almost all investment books written for the typical investor either skip this topic entirely or use incorrect comparisons (incorrect because there's always so much going on in the economy, thus the stock market, that simplistic comparisons – such as a comparison between the past and today – are essentially meaningless) and/with incomplete models, such as models based on P/E ratio, as we will soon see. *What is needed is something more sophisticated, yet complete, accurate, and relatively easy to use.*

In Chapter 5, I present an original table (there is a formula too, but reading the table is easier and I expect most investors to use the table) and criterion that will help answer the final question. While you won't get an exact answer, you will have an unequivocally correct comparison. Moreover, if you want to develop this further into a precise answer – and are willing to put in some work, sometimes too much work, unfortunately, because some companies have very messy financials – I include a couple of heuristics that you can use.

Unsurprisingly, my method involves current P/E ratio. However, unlike many methods that you will see elsewhere that just stop there (incorrectly), my method involves payout ratio and growth rate in earnings as well, in effect, *a nod, as there should be, to the underlying business characteristics and, in totality (with slight nudges), representing all three constituents of investor return, a very good sign!*

One final point, that I demonstrate with a real-world example: *Do not believe the hype that it is the dividend or dividend yield that is the reason you should invest for the long term in a dividend growth stock. Instead, almost always, the primary reason is the company's growth rate in earnings per share.*

To summarize, here is your fifth, and final, dividend growth lesson: **Estimate your stock's long-term return correctly.** ♣

5. Friday – The Right Kind of Magic

"Weather forecast for tonight: dark."

George Carlin

Short-term forecasting is difficult – history has this uneasy habit of not always repeating in the way it once did. What was important in the past, gradually, imperceptibly, becomes unimportant. Conversely, what was unimportant becomes important. *Even if someone gets it right once, the market often proves them wrong later.* Most traders and investors guess. And history has often proved such guesses wrong.

Over a short period – a few weeks, a few months, or even a year – prices parade in a game of chance, the rolls of the market-pricing die not counting for much. Short-term returns are random.

> *Over a longer period – five years, ten years, or even more – returns reflect the underlying business. The market noise averages out. What remains is the signal, the traits of the underlying business.*

Though supporters of Modern Portfolio Theory may disagree, I believe returns over a longer period are *not* random. A distinction between short- and long-term returns is important. Short-term, returns are random. Long-term, I believe, not so much.

EVERYTHING'S RELATIVE – OR IS IT?

"In the business world, the rearview mirror is always clearer than the windshield." Warren Buffett

To value stocks, we do not guess and we do not use Ouija boards. We use *valuation models* – which, admittedly, if not used carefully are no different from guessing or using Ouija boards!

In any case, valuation models are of two primary types:

- *relative valuation models* – where we compare our stock to something else; and

- *absolute valuation models* – where we value our stock directly.

With relative valuation models, we consider our stock undervalued – *relative to that something else* – if it comes out ahead in the comparison.

With absolute valuation models, we calculate – either directly or indirectly – the stock's expected return; and invest if the risk-return profile is favorable.

Because we are ultimately interested in *expected return*, you can guess which class of models we will eventually use! But, first, let's see why relative valuation models, which are simpler, are not the bee's knees.

The most well-known category of relative valuation models uses P/E ratios. With these models, we compare our stock's P/E ratio to that of the market, its peers, or even itself in the past. We consider our stock undervalued relative to the comparison if its P/E ratio is lower. For example, if our stock's P/E ratio is 12 and the market's P/E ratio is 15, we consider our stock undervalued relative to the market.

P/E models may work when comparing a stable company to itself in the past. They may also work when comparing the market to itself in the past – assuming the market is stable. On the other hand, P/E models fail with cyclical companies. In fact, with cyclical companies, P/E ratio is *lowest* when the company is at its cyclical peak (and earnings are high) – and the stock is about to fall to reflect the upcoming downturn in the business. In other words, with cyclical companies, a low P/E ratio tells you the stock is *overvalued*, not undervalued. P/E models also often fail with rapidly growing companies. In general, P/E models fail when earnings per share is meager – so that P/E ratio makes little sense; and when earnings per share is zero or negative – so that P/E ratio is undefined.

Analysts often base their earnings per share estimates on momentum: If a company is doing well, they project it will do better. If a company is doing poorly, they project it will do worse. Though, at some level, this approach is logical – and understandable – it introduces a *bias* in the earnings per share estimates: If you use these estimates when the company is doing well, you overestimate. If you use these estimates when the company is doing poorly, you underestimate. Moreover, you will not catch turns in the business.

Because some businesses are notoriously unstable, earnings per share estimates for these companies are unreliable – and momentum-based estimates often make things worse. Any use of P/E models for these companies is unreliable.

More generally, like a puzzle with missing pieces, P/E models are incomplete. They have at least two common shortcomings: (1) they do not account for growth; and (2) they do not account for dividends.

Peter Lynch, the famed mutual fund manager, addressed these omissions in his bestselling book, *One Up on Wall Street*. For non-dividend-paying companies, he advocated the use of models that use – what has come to be known as – the PEG ratio. The PEG ratio is P/E ratio divided by earnings per share growth rate, G, in percentage points. For instance, a stock with a P/E ratio of 12 and a G of 10 percent has a PEG ratio of 12 / 10 or 1.2. Implicitly, most investors use a one-year earnings per share growth rate in this comparison. For longer-term investors, a longer-term earnings per share growth rate, (say) a five-year value, may be more suitable. Lynch considered PEGs of 0.5 or less, very positive; and PEGs of 2.0 or more, very negative.

Many investors believe that a PEG of 1.0 indicates a fairly valued stock. This rule of thumb has little justification. For it to be valid, P/E ratios have to, at a minimum, (ideally) be proportional to growth and must not depend on anything else. But the relationship of P/E ratios to growth is nonlinear; and P/E ratios depend on factors such as risk.

Instead, think of PEG models, in general, and the PEG rule of 1.0, in particular, as *heuristics*. A PEG of 1.0 is a demarcating line – but only if a stock's PEG is *far* below 1.0 or *far* above 1.0. Even then it is not always right – but at least now it has a *chance* of being in the right ballpark. (To be fair, the broad range of Lynch's criteria does seem to reflect this.)

For dividend-paying companies, Lynch tweaked the PEG ratio. Dividends reduce growth. Moreover, because dividend yield is part of return, it cannot be excluded when considering returns, even indirectly. It seems natural therefore to compare P/E ratio to the sum of dividend yield (Y) and earnings per share growth rate (again, G), both in percentage points. Both Y and G are components of return and the ratio now treats them equally. *Moreover, the ratio now snuggles up to all three terms in the return equation of Chapter 3, a positive sign.* Let us call this ratio, the PEYG ratio. Lynch considered PEYGs of 0.5 or below attractive and PEYGs of 1.0 or above unattractive. For the unattractive criterion, he used 1.0, not the 2.0 that he used for PEGs.

Let's test the PEYG criteria with two examples. First, let's consider the market. Because the market's *current* P/E ratio has averaged about 14, the market's dividend yield has averaged about 3.0 percent, and the market's earnings per share growth rate has averaged about 6.5 percent, the market's PEYG ratio has averaged about 14 / (3.0 + 6.5) or 1.5. Thus, assuming we can apply the PEYG criteria to the market, the market has been anything but fairly valued, on average – an extremely dubious, and clearly incorrect, long-term conclusion.

Next, consider Johnson & Johnson. In early 2018, the stock traded at $140.23. The P/E ratio was 19.3. The dividend yield was 2.4 percent. Assuming a G of 6.5 percent, the PEYG ratio was 19.3 / (2.4 + 6.5) or 2.2. Because this exceeded 1.0 (by a wide margin), the PEYG model implied the stock was "unattractive." But extremes of 0.5 to 1.0 still create a *very* wide range: A PEYG ratio of 0.5 corresponds to a stock price of $49 and a PEYG ratio of 1.0 corresponds to a stock price of $78. Not only does this suggest that the stock is *vastly* overvalued, just as disconcerting, the range of stock prices, $49 to $78, is wide enough to drive a Hummer through.

In general, as with PEG models, think of PEYG models as heuristics. Both models fail when P/E ratio and G are meager, zero, or negative.

Another category of relative valuation models uses P/S ratios. P/S ratio is price per share divided by sales per share. With these models, we compare our stock's P/S ratio to the P/S ratio of other stocks, including peers, or even itself in the past. We consider our stock undervalued relative to the comparison if its P/S ratio is lower. Thus, for example, if our stock's P/S ratio is 1.25, and that of a peer is 1.50, we consider our stock undervalued relative to the peer.

P/S models do not account for profitability. A company can generate enormous sales by acting like Santa Claus – giving away its products, with or without red ribbons and wrapping paper. Based on its P/S ratio, it will look cheap. But without profits, unless the company regularly comes to the market for money, it will not survive for long. *Because of an emphasis on the top line, sales, and no accounting for the bottom line, profits; or in general, returns to shareholders, be wary of P/S models.* Although they may help spot very overvalued companies (P/S ratios more than (say) 10, for instance) and very cheap companies (P/S ratios less than (say) 0.2, for instance), you will find exceptions even here. In general, do *not* use P/S models.

Of the four models mentioned here – P/E, PEG, PEYG, and P/S models – P/E and PEYG models *may* apply to our dividend growth stocks – when comparing these companies to themselves in the past.

Still, relative valuation has many problems:

• The stock must resemble its comparison in all important details.

- None of the models (directly) account for risk. Ignoring risk is risky.

- *Relative valuation never tells you whether your stock is overvalued or undervalued.* It only tells you that your stock is *relatively* overvalued or *relatively* undervalued. During the late 1990s NASDAQ Bubble, one Internet stock may have looked undervalued relative to another. In fact, as it turned out, over a reasonable time frame, *all* were overvalued.

- Relative valuation makes more sense when you *hedge*, where, for instance, you buy the cheaper stock and short the more expensive comparison. In this case, it does not matter, essentially, that you do not know the ultimate value of a particular stock – as you are simply comparing, playing off one against the other. It is an open question whether it makes sense when you do not hedge, which will often be the case for most individual investors – who typically do not short.

T. S. Eliot once quipped, "it's not wise to violate rules until you know how to observe them." Likewise, *because of the many subtleties involved, use relative valuation only as a quick and dirty approach to valuation – and only as a start*. Appreciate the many pitfalls of its simplicity – simplicity that is almost impossible to defend. Do not apply relative valuation blindly.

ABSOLUTELY THE RIGHT IDEA

"Do not worry about your difficulties in Mathematics. I can assure you mine are still greater." Albert Einstein

In 1962, M. J. Gordon, working off earlier work by John Burr Williams in 1938, derived the granddaddy of the absolute valuation models, today called the Gordon Model or Gordon Growth Model. It features dividends prominently.

To produce the Gordon Model formula requires a three-step process (Figure 5.1): First, project the dividends (indefinitely), assuming

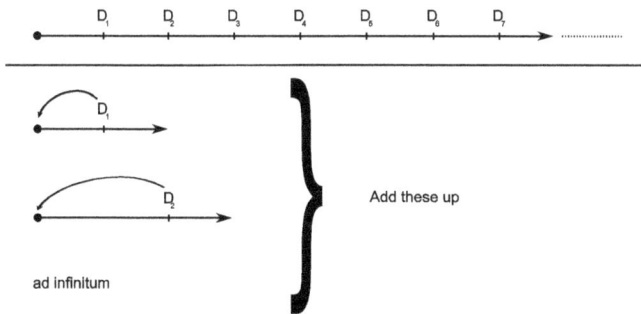

Figure 5.1: The Gordon Model, in conceptual terms, and without the mathematics: (1) Project the dividends (indefinitely), assuming they grow at a constant rate. (2) Discount each dividend to the present. (3) Add these up.

they grow at a constant rate. Second, discount each dividend to the present. Third, add these up. The constant dividend growth rate is a key feature of this model. It simplifies the mathematics.

The Gordon Model formula provided investors with deep insight at the time – the general principle remains undoubtedly correct. But the *direct* use of this model has problems that nullify its use for most companies today, including our dividend growth companies. (To be fair, its purpose may have always been to illustrate more than anything else.)

A MAGIC FORMULA

"The future is much like the present, only longer." Dan Quisenberry

The other day, while at Home Depot, I overheard one of the employees, who happened to be discussing investing with a customer, say, "Even if social security goes away, I'll be fine. I have $800,000 in my 401(k)." He seemed like just another Home Depot employee – though he likely had worked there for a while. There's something to be said for investing in good stocks for many, many years....

In my book, *Investing in Dividend Growth Stocks*, I develop an absolute valuation model to value dividend growth stocks involving a spreadsheet – perhaps a bit too much to ask of most investors. Here I emphasize – and *considerably* extend – an alternative approach, related to the spreadsheet but without using it explicitly, that I mentioned in passing in that book. It is not as precise but should be reasonable. (If you want to view or tinker with the spreadsheet, refer to the relevant links in the Notes section, starting on page 117, at the end of this chapter.)

We start with a *canonical* high-quality dividend growth stock with a return on beginning equity of 25 percent, higher than our required minimum of 20 percent. With a payout ratio of 65 percent, the company can grow at a sustainable rate of about 9 percent a year. I assume the company's markets and competition are such that the company can actually grow at this rate. Just to be careful, however, I reduce this growth rate for later years – after all, trees don't grow to the sky. Thus, I assume earnings growth rates (*not earnings per share growth rates!*) of 9 percent for Years 1-5, 9 percent for Years 6-10, 8 percent for Years 11-20, and 7 percent for Years 21-30 – leading to an average growth rate over the 30 years of 8 percent. I assume the business is stable – and do not reduce these rates further to account for earnings volatility. Years 31+ remains at 3 percent. Then the following formula – obtained from some mathematics and the spreadsheet (see my book, *Investing in Dividend Growth Stocks*, for details) – gives the canonical dividend growth stock's expected return in terms of its current P/E ratio, p:

$$-0.000828 * p^3 + 0.0625 * p^2 - 1.75 * p + 26.9$$

Yes, I know. Everyone *hates* formulas. And *this* is *ugly* – but it is no more than a sequence of basic arithmetic operations. Think about what you get in return: Just plug in the P/E ratio, and, abracadabra, you get the expected long-term return. You don't see this every day, do you? It's magic! Well, it isn't flying doves' kind of magic but it is cool. It solves a thorny little problem quickly and elegantly. You can use the magic formula for, roughly, a range of P/E ratios from 10 to 27.5.

In a real sense, the magic formula summarizes the book. Start with a company with a high internal return. Assume business stability so that internal return does not vary too much. With reasonable underlying market growth and allowing for slowing as the company ages,

Current P/E ratio	Expected return
10	14.8
11	14.1
12	13.5
13	12.9
14	12.4
15	11.9
16	11.5
17	11.1
18	10.8
19	10.5
20	10.3
21	10.0
22	9.8
23	9.6
24	9.5
25	9.3
26	9.1
27	8.9
27.5	8.8

Table 5.1: Using the magic formula. Use this table to read the expected return from the magic formula given a current P/E ratio. The expected return is in percent. The range of P/E ratios represent, roughly, the range of applicability of the magic formula.

calculate a payout ratio and deduce earnings growth rates. Then, the formula gives the return to expect. *Succinctly, the magic formula incorporates the business, return, and stability for a high-quality dividend growth stock.* I have this formula programmed into my HP-12C calculator that is more than twenty years old and is still reliably ticking. No joke – on both counts.

Nevertheless, I do want to make your investing life easier. Therefore, to simplify things, in Table 5.1, I show the expected return from the magic formula for a range of current P/E ratios. This should make it trivial to use the magic formula. Just look the result up.

But, wait, there's more! Even simpler, just remember the numbers below. They represent important demarcations:

- p/e ratio of 15, expected return of, roughly, 12 percent;

- p/e ratio of 21, expected return of 10 percent; and

- p/e ratio of 26, expected return of, roughly, 9 percent.

Or, roughly, in the context of historical stock market returns, (a current P/E ratio of) 15 or lower is excellent, 21 is reasonable, and 26 or higher is pricey.

You may argue that there isn't that much difference between a return of 9 percent a year and a return of 10 percent a year. For one year, that is fair. But remember, these are *long*-term returns. Over the long term, a difference of 1 percentage point a year is *huge*.

For the canonical dividend growth stock, a current P/E ratio of 21 or lower beats the market's long-term average of something less than 10 percent a year (depending on how far back you go, when you end, and so on). If you can achieve this return over the long term, you will be as set as that Home Depot employee with the $800,000 retirement account. Moreover, you will be *well* ahead of most individual investors, most mutual funds, and most ETFs – *and, very importantly, with typically much less risk, meaning you are far more likely to actually achieve this return than with the market or riskier stocks.*

Win, win, win. Egg rolls for everyone.

BENCHMARKING

"An approximate answer to the right question is worth a great deal more than a precise answer to the wrong question." John W. Tukey

I use the canonical dividend growth stock together with the magic formula directly or the associated table to *benchmark* other dividend growth stocks (and many other stocks as well, as long as they are reasonably stable). Here's how I do it:

- Calculate, or look up, the stock's current P/E ratio. (To calculate current P/E ratio, roughly, I use current stock price and earnings per share six months in the past plus six months in the future. You can get the earnings per share values from Value Line's *Investment Survey*, though Value Line uses a slightly different definition of earnings per share. If the quarters are off relative to my calculation date – for example, if the company's just completed quarter ended in June, and I am calculating current P/E ratio at the end of July – I make a small ad hoc adjustment.)

- Calculate the canonical dividend growth stock's expected return given this current P/E ratio – use the magic formula, or more simply, look up the return from Table 5.1, on page 97.

- If the stock resembles the canonical dividend growth stock, it will return the same. If it looks better, it will return more; if it looks worse, it will return less. To compare the company to the canonical dividend growth stock, I consider type of business, stability of earnings, return on beginning equity, growth rate in earnings, and payout ratio, though I often also quickly glance at debt, profit margin, and other such niceties.

That's it. All this takes just a few minutes. I keep things simple. For instance, if at the company's P/E ratio the expected return for the canonical dividend growth stock is low and I deem the stock worse than the canonical dividend growth stock, it will return less than what I consider a low return. End of story. Next!

Let's look at an example, PepsiCo, the company behind brands such as Pepsi and Frito Lay. I am not a fan of sugary drinks and I think the company, like Coca-Cola, has this giant problem of declining demand for such drinks, hindering long-term sales growth. In any case, as I write this, mid-2018, the company's current P/E ratio is 19. From Table 5.1, on page 97, the canonical dividend growth stock's expected return, given a current P/E ratio of 19, is 10.5 percent. Given PepsiCo's expected sluggish organic growth rate, I'd say the company is worse than the canonical dividend growth stock and, over the long term, should therefore return less than 10.5 percent a year. That's it. Done.

VALUATION

Though benchmarking is nice – and a good start – our ultimate goal is to *value* our dividend growth stocks (or even other stocks, as long as they are reasonably stable). To do this requires two steps. First, benchmark the stock as described above. Second, *quantitatively* take into account the differences between the stock and the canonical dividend growth stock. If the stock exhibits similar characteristics to that of the canonical dividend growth stock – identical average growth rate in earnings over the next 30 years and identical payout ratio – there's nothing further to do, its expected return matching the canonical dividend growth stock's expected return. If it differs, it's time to tinker.

As implied, the differences can arise in average growth rate in earnings over the next 30 years or payout ratio or both. In these circumstances, subject to an important caveat at the end of this section, make the following modifications to the canonical dividend growth stock's return:

For each percentage point higher than the canonical dividend growth stock's average growth rate in earnings over the next 30 years of 8 percent, increase the expected return 0.90 percentage points.

For each 5 percentage points higher than the canonical dividend growth stock's payout ratio of 65 percent, increase the expected return 0.40 percentage points.

Naturally, the other sides of these statements are also true, meaning, (1) for each percentage point *lower* than the canonical dividend growth stock's average growth rate in earnings over the next 30 years of 8 percent, *decrease* the expected return 0.90 percentage points, and (2) for each 5 percentage points *lower* than the canonical dividend growth stock's payout ratio of 65 percent, *decrease* the expected return 0.40 percentage points.

It can be confusing to remember all four variations. Just remember, higher is better and lower is worse: Thus, higher (lower) growth and higher (lower) payout ratios mean higher (lower) returns.

If you don't want to bother with all this math, here is a link to a webpage where I have coded the magic formula, and the above modifications, online. Enter three values, then press *Calculate!*:

http://www.neocadence.com/2018/10/valuing-dividend-growth-stock-with.html

Suppose you've benchmarked a stock and decided it should do worse than the canonical dividend growth stock. The stock has a P/E ratio of 20 and the canonical dividend growth stock with that P/E ratio returns 10.3 percent. Let's value it to see just how much worse. Suppose we expect the stock to have an average growth rate in earnings over the next 30 years of 5 percent and a payout ratio of 75 percent. Because average growth rate in earnings is 3 percentage points lower than the canonical dividend growth stock's, we decrease the canonical dividend growth stock's expected return 3 * 0.9 percentage points, or 2.7 percentage points. Because payout ratio is 10 percentage points higher than the canonical dividend growth stock's, we increase the expected return 2 * 0.4 percentage points, or 0.8 percentage points. Thus, because the canonical dividend growth stock's return is 10.3 percent, we expect the stock to return 10.3 - 2.7 + 0.8 percent, or 8.4 percent, a year.

Now, let's continue with PepsiCo from the previous section, where we decided that the stock would return less than the canonical dividend growth stock's return of 10.5 percent a year. PepsiCo's return on equity has soared in recent years, because of debt, to more than 65 percent. Its payout ratio (remember this is more than just dividends!) is likely in the 85 percent range. Very long-term estimates of *earnings per share* growth rate probably average about 6 percent, of which likely 2 percentage points are because of share buybacks. Thus, the company's *earnings* growth rate is about 4 percent (6 - 2, roughly). Because average growth rate in earnings is 4 percentage points lower than the canonical dividend growth stock's, I decrease the canonical dividend growth stock's expected return 4 * 0.9 percentage points, or 3.6 percentage points. Because payout ratio is 20 percentage points higher than the canonical dividend growth stock's, I increase the expected return 4 * 0.4 percentage points, or 1.6 percentage points. Thus, because the canonical dividend growth stock's return is 10.5 percent, I expect PepsiCo to return 10.5 - 3.6 + 1.6 percent, or 8.5 percent a year. This return meshes well with PepsiCo's return the last several years and the sum of its dividend yield and earnings per share growth, a near-term view of the return. So we are probably in the right ballpark. Now, if you want to be tougher or more conservative, depending on your viewpoint, you can shave another point off this return because of the long-term demand issues with sugary drinks. I know I would. Thus, 7.5 percent a year seems reasonable.

A few cautions: (1) Valuations are never fixed in stone. If conditions change – and they will – readjust, re-evaluate. (2) The more our stock differs from the canonical dividend growth stock, the higher the expected error – any result within a range of 0.5 percentage points must be considered fair. (3) I assume earnings growth rate ranges similar to the ranges in my spreadsheet, with earnings growth rates decreasing as the company gets older. Implicitly, therefore, I assume any stated average earnings growth rate incorporates earnings growth rates of R percent a year for 10 years, S percent a year for the next 10 years, and T percent a year for the last 10 years (of the 30), where R >= S >= T. (4) I base the heuristics above on playing with my spreadsheet model in my book, *Investing in Dividend Growth Stocks*, and trend lines. In particular, the heuristics are reasonably useful over a range of current P/E ratios of 15 to 24, payout ratios from 50 percent to 90 percent, and the moderate growth rates typical of our dividend growth stocks. As with *all* heuristics, do *not* treat these as sacrosanct.

YOUR TURN

It is worth taking the time to understand the benchmarking and valuation ideas well. Some practice will help. Please proceed in order as the questions build on themselves.

Please answer the following questions:

1. A dividend growth stock, XYZ, has a return on beginning equity of 20 percent. Its payout ratio is 60 percent. Its sustainable growth rate is

   a) 7 percent.

   b) 8 percent.

   c) 9 percent.

2. Suppose, over the next 30 years, XYZ grows earnings 8 percent the first decade, 7 percent the second decade, and 6 percent the

third decade. The average growth rate in earnings over the next
30 years is

a) 8 percent.

b) 7 percent.

c) 6 percent.

3. XYZ's current P/E ratio is 20. Using the magic formula or our
helpful table, the canonical dividend growth stock with this current P/E ratio has an expected return of

a) 10.3 percent.

b) 10.9 percent.

c) 11.3 percent.

4. XYZ is worse than the canonical dividend growth stock.

a) True.

b) False.

5. Thus, we expect XYZ to return more than the canonical dividend
growth stock.

a) True.

b) False.

6. Because XYZ's average growth rate in earnings over the next 30
years is 1 percentage point lower than the canonical dividend
growth stock's, decrease the canonical dividend growth stock's
expected return

a) 2 percentage points.

b) 1.5 percentage points.

c) 0.9 percentage points.

7. Because XYZ's payout ratio is 5 percentage points lower than
the canonical dividend growth stock's, decrease the canonical
dividend growth stock's expected return

a) 1.0 percentage points.

b) 0.4 percentage points.

c) 0.1 percentage points.

8. Using the answers to questions (3), (6), and (7), we expect XYZ to return

   a) 10.5 percent.

   b) 9 percent.

   c) 7.5 percent.

Answers:

1. (b)

2. (b)

3. (a)

4. (a)

5. (b)

6. (c)

7. (b)

8. (b)

ONE MORE

Now that you've got it, here's a complete valuation question (bench-marking included, implicitly):

> Suppose a dividend growth stock, RST, has a return on be-ginning equity of 25 percent. Its payout ratio is 70 percent. Suppose over the next 30 years, RST grows earnings 7 per-cent the first decade, 6 percent the second decade, and 5 percent the third decade. RST's current P/E ratio is 15. What is RST's expected return?

The answer is in the Notes section, starting on page 117, at the end of this chapter.

IS OUR MODEL COMPLETE?

"Financial genius is before the fall." John Kenneth Galbraith.

You may have seen the occasional investment TV personality point to the graph of a stock on a screen and project its stock price based on some version of a pair of trend lines, a channel. They might say, "Well, see how the stock sits in this channel? It keeps rising but always sits between this line and that line. Thus, once it hits the lower line, buy. Once it hits the upper line, sell. It really is that simple!"

What's wrong with this picture? *Quite simply, there is absolutely no justification for the stock price to maintain the channel in the future.* If you look at enough stocks, you will be able to fit *some* sort of model to at least a few of them, *purely by chance*. In this case, the model is a channel. But why would the stock continue to respect this channel? *There's no earthly reason why it should. The model is deficient, incomplete, because it fails to establish an* **honest** *reason why the stock should remain in the channel in the future – there has to be a logically consistent and complete rationale.* (One rationale is, well everyone does it so there's your reason. That's possible, but it is still not quite an honest reason. It is still very much based on faith.)

As noted, the magic formula is based on a spreadsheet model from my earlier book, *Investing in Dividend Growth Stocks*. In turn, this model depends on just three factors: assumed payout ratio, growth rates (of earnings), and current P/E ratio. But do we have the right stuff?

In *any* first principles mathematical analysis of the value of something, we need the amounts, the timing of those amounts, and a rate to discount those amounts to the present. (Compare these requirements to those of the Gordon Model. They are one and the same.) We have the amounts, the payouts. We have the timing, once a year going into the far future. We do not have the rate, but effectively we *back* into it by seeing what return is *built* into the current stock price. Thus, we have a complete model.

You may have noticed one slight problem, however. Theoretically, we have to use the *exact* amounts at each point in time. We do not. Instead, we use a reasonable estimate of what the company can, and should, pay. This gets us past the thorny problem of having to understand and project every company nuance. Over a short period, we will invariably be off. But this book is not about the short term. It

is about the long term. And in this case, although we will still likely
have the exact amounts wrong, as long as we are close enough, especially in the aggregate, we should be all right – as regards the *long-term*
expected return. (In this regard, we are helped by the *stability* of dividend growth stocks. It would be quite a different matter – and wrong
– to reach the same conclusion if the stock had represented a volatile
business. The spreadsheet, as is, that is without, admittedly not very
difficult, further modification, would not work.)

Note that our approach differs from approaches that use just one
variable – for example, relative valuation approaches that use (say) a
multiple of earnings per share. *Models such as these are always going
to be incomplete.* In other words, two stocks may have the same P/E
ratio – leading one to conclude they will return the same – but, more
often than not, returns will differ. Models such as these are akin to
touching just a part of the elephant – and reaching conclusions that
will be right, at best, purely by chance. Most often, the conclusions,
if they are stated to any reasonable precision, will be wrong. User
beware.

HOW HAVE WE DONE?

*"We believe that a fundamental measure of our success will be the shareholder
value that we create over the **long term** [emphasis added]." Jeff Bezos*

*"Year, n. A period of three hundred and sixty-five disappointments." Am-
brose Bierce*

In the print edition of my earlier book, *Investing in Dividend Growth
Stocks*, I listed twenty dividend growth stocks to consider (Table 5.2).
Taken as a portfolio, these stocks have soundly outperformed the mar-
ket.

Assume that on 31 December 2007, an investor had put $1,000 into
each of the twenty and $20,000 in the S&P 500® index. Dividends are
reinvested. Figure 5.2 shows the subsequent performance. As of 31
December 2017, the $20,000 in the index was worth $45,245. Not bad.
But the portfolio of twenty knocked the cover off the ball. As of 31
December 2017, the $20,000 in the portfolio was worth $83,208, more
than *quadruple* the initial investment. In terms of annual returns, the
index returned a very typical long-term market-averaging 8.5 percent

Accenture	McCormick
Clorox	McDonald's
Colgate-Palmolive	Nike
Donaldson Company	Papa John's
Emerson Electric	Parker-Hannifin
FactSet	Praxair
Genuine Parts	Ross Stores
Graco	TJX Companies, The
Honeywell	United Technologies
Johnson & Johnson	Valspar

Table 5.2: Twenty dividend growth stocks to consider from my book, *Investing in Dividend Growth Stocks*, print edition. Valspar was subsequently acquired.

a year – while the portfolio of twenty returned a stunning 15.3 percent a year. And, because dividend growth stocks are relatively conservative, the twenty did so with less risk – a considerably unappreciated aspect of all forms of investing – meaning you are *far* more likely to actually *achieve* this return than you would otherwise with the market or riskier stocks. (Companies experience business risk and valuation risk. With our dividend growth stocks, business risk is relatively low, so it is only a matter of valuation risk. This sort of dance is much trickier with many other stocks. For more details about risk, please see my book, *Investing in Dividend Growth Stocks*.)

The portfolio also beat the market over the last 1, 3, 5, 7, and 10 years (Table 5.3). However, it would be remiss of me to not point out that 1 year and even 3 years is *much too short* of an *investing* time frame. Contrary to the rapid trading tendencies of most of today's mutual funds, and many investors, *investing of any form* is almost by definition a long-term process. *It makes almost no sense to consider such short periods!*

In certain markets – strong markets and frothy markets – dividend growth stocks underperform. On the other hand, in every other kind of market, dividend growth stocks typically outperform. In fact, in the worst possible markets – disastrous markets, for example, the Crash of 2008 – they significantly outperform.

The stocks in the portfolio have done even better than this. In Table

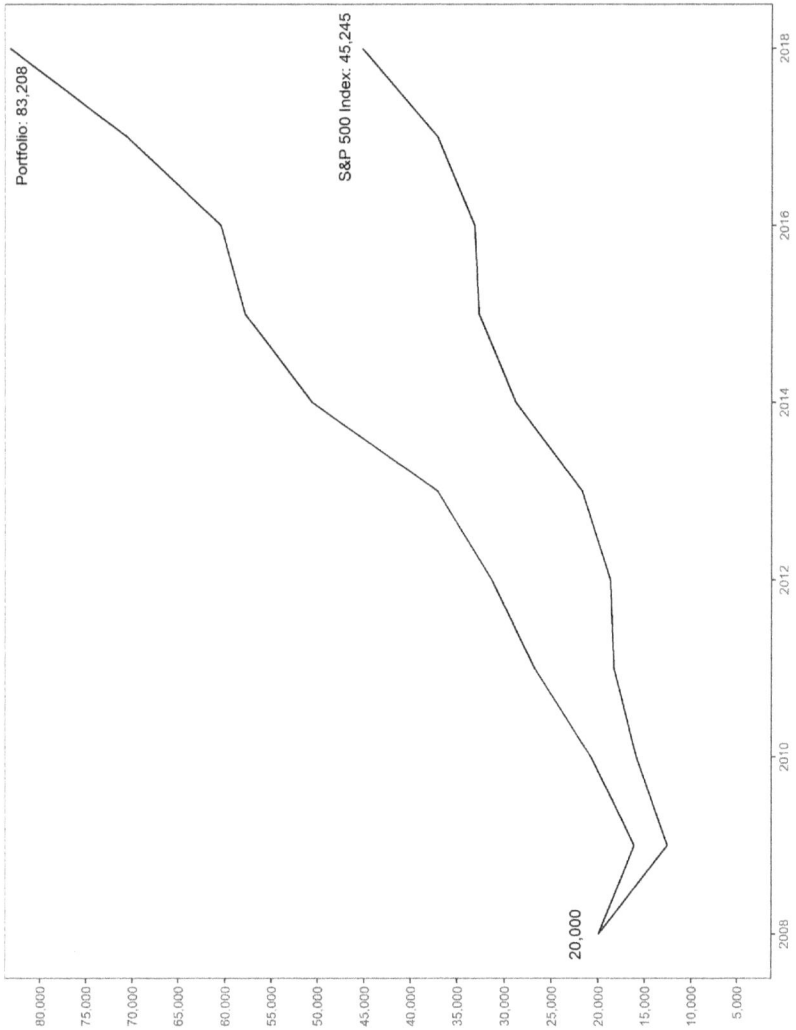

Figure 5.2: Portfolio of twenty dividend growth stocks from my book, *Investing in Dividend Growth Stocks*, print edition, versus the S&P 500 index. $20,000 is invested in the portfolio – equally divided among the twenty, $1,000 in each stock – and the S&P 500 index on 31 December 2007. (I do not include possible spinoffs, and other corporate actions, for the stocks in my book's portfolio, thus possibly underestimating a stock's return, thus, the portfolio's return. As Valspar was acquired, the Valspar balance was split evenly among the remaining stocks on 31 December 2016.) The final portfolio and index amounts are as of 31 December 2017. Dividends are reinvested.

Period	Cumulative Portfolio Return	Cumulative S&P 500 Index Return
1 Year	**23.2%**	21.8%
3 Years	**43.6%**	38.3%
5 Years	**116.8%**	108.2%
7 Years	**195.5%**	146.6%
10 Years	**316.0%**	126.2%

Table 5.3: Cumulative portfolio return of twenty dividend growth stocks from my book, *Investing in Dividend Growth Stocks*, print edition, versus the cumulative return of the S&P 500 index over different periods. (I do not include possible spinoffs, and other corporate actions, for the stocks in my book's portfolio, thus possibly underestimating a stock's return, thus, the portfolio's return. As Valspar was acquired, the Valspar balance was split evenly among the remaining stocks on 31 December 2016.) Each period ends on 31 December 2017. Dividends are reinvested. The better performance for each period is shown in **bold**.

5.4, I compare the average (annual) return of a stock in the portfolio to the annual return of the S&P 500 index. Dividends are reinvested. Nine times out of ten, the stocks in the portfolio beat the index. Ninety percent is, quite simply, hitting it out of the ballpark. This table also highlights the consistency of the portfolio – it outperforms regularly. In other words, the portfolio did not just benefit from some unusual and lucky happenstance.

Honestly, it does not get a whole lot better than this, especially when accounting for risk.

But what creates this magic? You will not be surprised when I say, the business. Quite simply, these business traits do the trick:

- a good internal return such as a long-run return on beginning equity average of twenty percent or more;

- the sustainability of this internal return; and

- stable, moderate underlying market growth.

Year	Average Return of a Stock in Portfolio	S&P 500 Index Return
2008	**-19.3%**	-37.0%
2009	**29.5%**	26.5%
2010	**29.0%**	15.1%
2011	**14.4%**	2.1%
2012	**17.9%**	16.0%
2013	**36.0%**	32.4%
2014	11.8%	**13.7%**
2015	**1.9%**	1.4%
2016	**17.0%**	12.0%
2017	**23.2%**	21.8%

Table 5.4: Average annual return of a stock in the portfolio of twenty dividend growth stocks from my book, *Investing in Dividend Growth Stocks*, print edition, versus the annual return of the S&P 500 index. (I do not include possible spinoffs, and other corporate actions, for the stocks in my book's portfolio, thus possibly underestimating a stock's return. Valspar was acquired and is excluded from the 2017 calculation.) Dividends are reinvested. The better performance in each year is shown in **bold**.

Because of the first and third traits, the company returns a reasonable amount of cash to shareholders as share buybacks and dividends. Because of the second and third, the company generates stable, modestly growing profits. Profits are not erratic. They do not collapse. Moreover, stable, modestly growing profits form the basis of dividend growth. Because of all three traits, (business) risk is relatively low.

In turn, stock prices express similar traits. They show stable growth. They generally do not crumble. Complete failure is rare. Shareholders benefit from the steady compounding of stable, moderate, and sustainable returns.

DRIVERS

Turning next to individual stock performance, what drives *multiyear* returns for dividend growth stocks? Is it dividend yield? P/E ratio? Donuts? In Figure 5.3, I show the drivers of multiyear return for a prototypical dividend growth stock, Colgate-Palmolive. In this case,

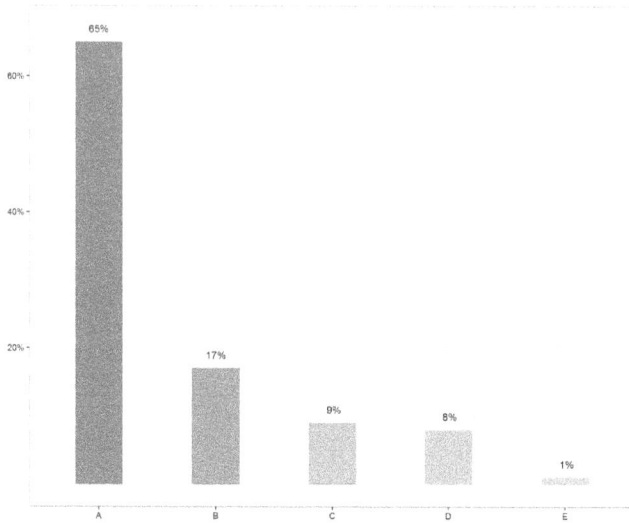

Figure 5.3: Contributions to exact multiyear return for Colgate-Palmolive. The period covers the ten fiscal years through 31 December 2015. Dividends are reinvested. The separation is rough. It assumes, for instance, that dividends are paid at the middle of the ten-year period. The contributions are grouped, A to E. A is growth rate in earnings per share. B is continuation of initial dividend yield. C is combination of growth rate in earnings per share and other factors. D is growth rate in P/E ratio. E is growth rate in dividend payout ratio. *Growth rate in earnings per share is the primary driver of multiyear return. It is not even close. It dominates everything else.*

growth rate in earnings per share, *by itself*, drives a whopping *65* percent of multiyear return. (And there's a bit more. Growth rate in earnings per share gets further credit by virtue of its interplay with other factors. I do not include this contribution in the 65 percent.) By contrast, initial dividend yield drives just 17 percent of multiyear return.

Though there are some caveats, I have found similar patterns with the vast majority of dividend growth stocks: *growth rate in earnings per share drives the majority of long-term return*. This domination arises because growth rate in earnings per share is relatively large. Over long periods, because of the magic of compounding, it absolutely dominates.

By contrast, some investors have a, perhaps understandable, infatuation with dividends. *In general, however, dividends only help confirm underlying business stability – or they should anyway.* They should *not* be the primary focus when it comes to return for our dividend growth stocks – and return should always be *your* most important focus!

In general, for our dividend growth stocks:

- *Do not view dividend yield as the primary driver of return, even when dividends are reinvested.*

- *Do reinvest your dividends. Over long periods, the gains from reinvestment do almost as much heavy lifting as the dividends themselves.*

To summarize, when you consider your dividend growth stocks, pay attention to expected growth rate in earnings per share. It is more important than dividends. Ideally, you want this growth to be moderate (8-12 percent a year for large-caps, 8-16 percent a year for midcaps) and stable. Regarding stability, twenty percent one year and two percent the next does not cut it. In this case, the market rewards the stock when growth soars; then summarily pummels the stock when growth falls. Net, because of the mathematical implications of higher volatility, multiyear compound returns plummet, implying your wealth does not rise nearly as much as it would have had growth been more stable.

DATA

Use the following sources for data. The first three are broadly applicable:

Value Line, *http://www.valueline.com*

SEC EDGAR, *https://goo.gl/bKxLAo*, the company search page

General-purpose finance websites (for example, a popular site is Yahoo! Finance, *http://finance.yahoo.com*)

The fourth is company-specific:

Company investor relations websites, (for example, as of mid-2018, for McCormick, *https://goo.gl/XdQN41*)

Value Line's *Investment Survey* is *indispensable* for historical financial data on large companies. I consider the *Investment Survey* a must-read for long-term investors and I highly recommend it. It is available at most libraries, if not as a printed copy, then at least online. (You can read a sample Value Line report here: *https://goo.gl/x2y721*. If you are not used to these reports, refer to the following, How to read a Value Line research report: *https://goo.gl/m0rR5X*.)

As of mid-2018, you will find the following items on each stock's *Investment Survey* page useful for dividend growth investing:

- Header, for stock price, P/E ratio, and dividend yield;

- Business, for a description of the company;

- Earnings per share;

- Dividends declared per share;

- Common shares outstanding;

- Net profit;

- Net profit margin;

- Long-term debt;

- Return on shareholders' equity;

- All dividends to net profit;

- Capital structure;

- (Estimated) annual rates of change (per share) of earnings and dividends.

Use the SEC's EDGAR database to search for company filings. Read the filings to understand what a company does, learn about its business risks, and access its financial statements. Like shoulder checks, it is always good practice to read a company's SEC EDGAR filings before you invest. General-purpose finance websites are good for a host of company data, though, of course, quantity and quality does vary.

Investor relations websites are useful for events, presentations, dividend histories, annual reports, and links to SEC EDGAR filings. Some investor relations websites have useful overview documents that explain how the business works.

This chapter completes the book's theory and occasional sampling. Over the weekend, in the next chapter, we get to put everything into practice, looking at several examples. By the end of that chapter, *you'll* be the expert. Onward!

Quiz

1. Short-term forecasting is difficult.

    a) True.
    b) False.

2. P/E models are incomplete.

    a) True.
    b) False.

3. A PEG of 1.0 indicates a fairly valued stock.

    a) True.
    b) False.

4. P/S models do not account for

    a) sales.
    b) price.
    c) profitability.

5. The Gordon Model can be used to value most stocks today.

    a) True.
    b) False.

6. Our canonical stock has a return on beginning equity of

    a) 15 percent.
    b) 25 percent.
    c) 35 percent.

7. According to the magic formula, a current P/E ratio of 21 is reasonable.

   a) True.
   b) False.

8. According to the magic formula, a current P/E ratio of 30 is pricey.

   a) True.
   b) False.

9. You can use the magic formula as a benchmark for stable stocks.

   a) True.
   b) False.

10. In valuing a dividend growth stock, if the stock has an average growth rate in earnings over the next 30 years of 9 percent we must increase the canonical dividend growth stock's expected return

   a) 10 percentage points.
   b) 5 percentage points.
   c) 0.9 percentage points.

11. In valuing a dividend growth stock, if the stock has a payout ratio of 65 percent we must decrease the canonical dividend growth stock's expected return

   a) 0 percentage points.
   b) 0.4 percentage point.
   c) 0.8 percentage points.

12. Our model to value dividend growth stocks is complete.

   a) True.
   b) False.

13. For our dividend growth stocks, growth rate in earnings per share drives the majority of long-term return.

   a) True.
   b) False.

ANSWERS

1. (a)

2. (a)

3. (b)

4. (c)

5. (b)

6. (b)

7. (a)

8. (a)

9. (a)

10. (c)

11. (a)

12. (a)

13. (a)

WHISPERS

- Over a longer period – five years, ten years, or even more – returns reflect the underlying business. The market noise averages out. What remains is the signal, the traits of the underlying business.

- Valuation models are of two primary types: relative valuation models and absolute valuation models.

- P/E models are incomplete. They have at least two common shortcomings: (1) they do not account for growth; and (2) they do not account for dividends.

- Because of the many subtleties involved, use relative valuation only as a quick and dirty approach to valuation – and only as a start.

- Our magic formula incorporates the business, return, and stability for a high-quality dividend growth stock.

- Roughly, in the context of historical stock market returns, from our magic formula, a current P/E ratio of 15 or lower is excellent (leading to expected returns of roughly 12 percent of more), 21 is reasonable (an expected return of 10 percent), and 26 or higher is pricey (expected returns of roughly 9 percent or less).

- Use heuristics to adjust the magic formula for a different average growth rate in earnings over the next 30 years (a 0.90 percentage point increase in expected return for each percentage point that the average growth rate in earnings over the next 30 years is higher than the canonical dividend growth stock's 8 percent) and a different payout ratio (a 0.40 percentage point increase in expected return for each 5 percentage points that the stock's payout ratio is higher than the canonical dividend growth stock's payout ratio of 65 percent).

- For our dividend growth stocks, growth rate in earnings per share drives the majority of long-term return.

NOTES

- The problems with the Gordon Model fall into two categories:

    Inflexible dividend growth rates: (a) The dividend growth rate has to be constant. But no company grows at one rate forever. Growth rates change. Typically, a company's growth rate slows as it ages. (b) Even with a constant dividend growth rate, it cannot be too large. For instance, it cannot exceed the growth rate of the economy. If it did, the company would one day become the economy. (c) The formula cannot be used – it does not apply – when dividend growth rate equals or exceeds expected return.
    Inflexible amounts: (a) Not all companies pay dividends. (b) The formula implicitly requires that companies pay the maximum possible as dividends. Few do.

- You can download a copy of the spreadsheet by typing this link into your web browser: *https://goo.gl/Eo9gTj*. I created the spreadsheet in Windows 7 using Excel 7. Thus, in an ideal world, you have the same or compatible operating system and spreadsheet application – and the link, which depends on Google Drive (and Google URL Shortener), continues to work. As an alternative, the following link will let you at least view the spreadsheet (in Google Sheets): *https://goo.gl/9kWaVm*. If you do this, you will notice that I do not make the file editable. Thus, one errant entry by one person does not spoil it for everyone else. Once you have the spreadsheet open, you may be able to download it as an Excel or other spreadsheet. Google Sheets ruins the original formatting. If this happens to you, you will need to tidy things up. Using the spreadsheet is easy. Typically, you enter the stock ticker and eight numbers – the stock price and seven estimates, four of which are (related) growth rates – and out jumps the answer. For more details, refer to my book, *Investing in Dividend Growth Stocks*.

- Regarding the magic formula, because I assume growth rate falls as the company ages – but payout ratio remains the same – I implicitly assume return of beginning equity falls with age. Some companies ratchet up return of beginning equity as they age by taking on excessive debt, for instance. This extra debt makes them riskier. I choose to be more conservative – implying, ideally, that the returns that the companies *actually* generate are somewhat higher than the returns I calculate. That's the hope anyway.

- You may wonder why I do not simply use the earnings per share growth rate instead of the earnings growth rate in the magic formula. Because doing so would mean including share buybacks twice – indirectly in a boosted earnings per share growth rate and directly in the payout ratio. That's double-counting, a no-no. Then you may ask, well, why not use the dividend payout ratio instead of the payout ratio and incorporate share buybacks as a higher earnings per share growth rate? Theoretically, that would work – and should give you the same answer. However, I believe getting the cash payouts wrong – and hoping to paper this over with other details such as a higher earnings per share growth rate – gets you into a heap of trouble. It all boils down to the sensitivity of the model, these types of models being quite sensitive to the growth rates. In my opinion, that's where many mistakes occur, subtle ones at that. Because of the many moving parts, valuation is a non-trivial exercise. Here, I try to get one big thing right – or as right as I possibly can – the very important cash payouts. Doing so very likely leads to much better results as the cash payouts I use are much closer to (a normalized version of) free cash flow, especially these days as companies continue to favor the flexibility of share buybacks over the rigidity of dividends, with share buybacks consequently constituting a rising portion of the cash returned to shareholders.

- To gauge the validity of the magic formula, I compared the average expected return of the twenty dividend growth stocks to consider from my book, *Investing in Dividend Growth Stocks*, to the average expected return as calculated here. The average expected return for the twenty – as stated in the book – is 10.72 percent. The method here produces an average expected return of 10.8 percent. That's more than close enough.

- The answer to the valuation question posed in the One More section, on page 104, is 10.5 percent. At a current P/E ratio of 15, using the magic formula or our helpful table, the canonical dividend growth stock has an expected return of 11.9 percent. RST's average growth rate in earnings over the next 30 years is 6 percent. Because 6 percent is 2 percentage points lower than the canonical dividend growth stock's, lower the canonical dividend growth stock's expected return 2 * 0.9 percentage points, or 1.8 percentage points. Because RST's payout ratio is 5 percentage points higher than the canonical dividend growth stock's, increase the canonical dividend growth stock's expected return 0.4 percentage points. Thus, we expect RST to return 11.9 - 1.8 + 0.4 percent, or 10.5 percent, a year. ♣

Making a List, Checking it Twice

"The Tao abides in non-action, yet nothing is left undone."   *Lao-tzu*

Here is a checklist to quickly evaluate any dividend growth stock. If a stock fails to meet a key requirement on this checklist, stop and consider whether the miss can be excused; or stop, turn the page, and consider something else.

Here is the checklist (the items in square brackets are important but perhaps slightly less so than the rest – not all good dividend growth stocks meet these particular requirements):

1. Does the business make sense?

    a) Stable or falling competition.
    b) Stable, modestly growing profits.
    c) [Ideally, share counts fall 1-2 percent a year.]
    d) Reasonable risks.

2. Do the financials confirm the story?

    a) [Profit margins are good or strong. Currently, mid-2018, ten to fifteen percent is good and more than fifteen percent is strong.]
    b) Moderate financial leverage.
    c) *A long-run return on beginning equity average of twenty percent or more.*

3. Does the payout ratio signal the right maturity?

    a) A payout ratio that averages at least fifty percent.

4. Is expected growth reasonable?

    a) Moderate expected five-year earnings per share growth rates, namely 8-12 percent a year for large companies and 8-16 percent a year for midsize companies.

5. Never pay too much.

    a) Value the stock correctly. Use the magic formula (or associated table) plus heuristic adjustments. Buy the stock if you feel the expected return is fair, ideally above market with lower than average risk (a combination that some purists would find shocking – just ignore them and carry on!).

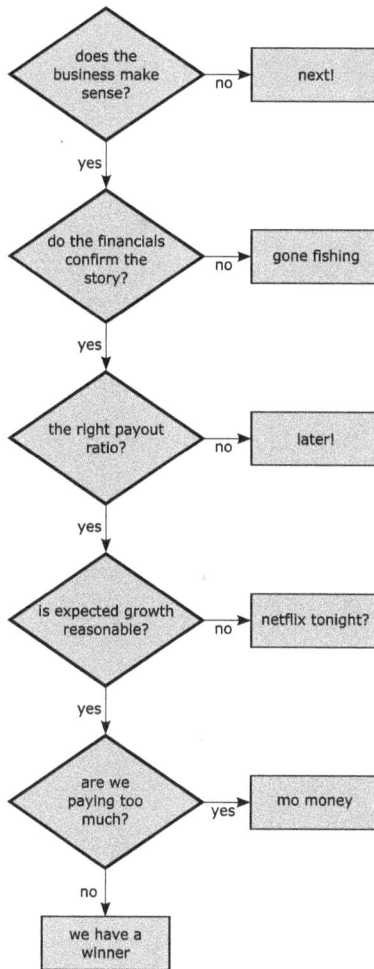

Figure C.1: Checklist: Decisions, Decisions

That's it (Figure C.1)!

As with any discipline or problem that you understand properly, if you focus on the right things, it all becomes exceptionally simple – and, if done correctly, the above checklist and a bit of patience can generate very strong long-term investment results and outstanding investment success. ♣

Prelude to Chapter 6

"I tell you Wellington is a bad general, the English are bad soldiers; we will settle this matter by lunch time."   *Napoleon Bonaparte*

Many books that profess to make you a better investor end up leaving you hanging – like a Tom Brady high-five. There's lots of rah-rah talk and fist-pumping – marketing sells – but not much else. In fact, in many cases, I sense the books merely *pretend* to cover the material, many books containing an abundance of mistakes and omissions, some subtle, some glaring, others good at rehashing old platitudes but not doing much else. Especially as it relates to investing, a little knowledge, or the wrong "knowledge," *is* a dangerous thing.

I wrote this book to distill the core ideas behind investing in dividend growth stocks correctly – but, ultimately, I want *you* to become a successful investor. In this regard, examples do help. In Chapter 6, we apply what we have learned. We apply the checklist to several dividend growth stocks.

The sources for much of the information here are recent company presentations and annual reports. Regarding annual reports, especially read through the sections on *Business, Competition,* and *Risk Factors.* For much of the numerical background, see the section, *Selected Financial Data.* For example, for Nike, see *https://goo.gl/HNyVdm.* For the payout ratio, I use the *Statement of Cash Flows,* the third of the three key financial statements that companies produce – but because undertaking this can be tricky for those not used to reading financial statements, I offer an alternative. For the latest dividend and share buyback news, search the company's press releases. Stock prices are available on Yahoo! Finance, of course, or the company website as well. Quarterly and annual earnings per share are on Yahoo! Finance.

You can analyze everything *much* faster using Value Line. With Value Line, you see a longer history at a glance. Value Line is a one-stop shop for our kind of analysis.

One important point: Earnings for many companies have benefited *tremendously* from the recent lowering of the corporate tax rate, earnings and many other metrics *spontaneously* rising. As a result, in some ways, the past is not necessarily prologue.

Finally, you will notice that not all these stocks meet all our requirements precisely. That's just the way it goes. The real world is often messy. We just have to compromise correctly.

Here we go. Last one, fast one. ♣

6. The Weekend – Examples

"Do, or do not. There is no try."
                    Yoda (The Empire Strikes Back)

Two Bugaboos

The two annoyances with my approach to valuation are figuring out the earnings (not earnings per share!) growth rate and figuring out the payout ratio, the latter a considerably larger annoyance.

You can calculate the earnings growth rate two ways: (1) Because earnings per share data is more commonly available than earnings data, the simplest way, though a bit rough, is to take the earnings per share growth rate and subtract the share buyback rate. For example, if a company has an average earnings per share growth rate of 10 percent a year the last 10 years, but has bought back shares at an average rate of 1.5 percent a year over that period, its earnings growth rate is 10 - 1.5 or 8.5 percent a year. As a shortcut to determining the share buyback rate, a 10 percent reduction in share count over 10 years implies, roughly, a share count reduction of 1 percent a year; a 20 percent reduction in share count over 10 years implies, roughly, a share count reduction of 2.2 percent a year; and a 30 percent reduction in share count over 10 years implies, roughly, a share count reduction of 3.5 percent a year. Sometimes, companies accelerate their share buybacks with a large amount of debt. Be aware of that as, theoretically, they should not get full credit in the calculation for this. (2) The more direct way is to use earnings. For instance, suppose a company grew earnings from 100 to 110 to 133. (I'm using 3 years for simplicity, here. Ideally use a long time frame, say 11 years of earnings to get 10 growth rates.) Its growth rates are (110 - 100) / 100 or 10 percent and (133 - 110) / 110 or 20 percent, respectively. The average is (10 + 20) / 2 or 15 percent a year. (For a more sophisticated take, use a mathematical trick called (exponential) regression to work out the growth rates, though this can sound like Greek if you are unfamiliar with the concept or don't have access to Excel or similar software – I often used regression to create the values in the examples here. In general, do not use compound average growth rates as doing so gives undue importance to the first and last values.)

You can find the data that you need in Value Line's *Investment Survey*. For earnings, refer to the "Net Profit" row. For earnings per share growth rate, refer to "Earnings", "Past 10 Yrs.", in the "Annual Rates" box. For share counts, refer to the "Common Shares Outstanding" row. You can also get all the information that you need from company annual reports, though this can be considerably more painful because you'll have to search through many.

Incidentally, with growth rates in *earnings*, our criteria for the expected five-year earnings *per share* growth rate – 8-12 percent for a large-cap and 8-16 percent for a midcap – shift *downward*, the degree of shift depending on the size and effectiveness of the share buyback. Do not be alarmed, therefore, by growth rates in earnings of less than 8 percent in the examples here.

Turning to the payout ratio, this one can be a real beast. In general, I would advise those of you unaccustomed to reading financial statements to do the calculations a few times, say, with payout ratios of 60 percent, 70 percent, and 80 percent. To calculate the payout ratio more carefully, see the appendix to this chapter, on page 169.

Now, with these preliminaries over, let's get to the fun part – the examples!

ACCENTURE

Accenture (ticker: ACN) is a massive, global (technology) professional services company, operating in 53 countries, and "providing a broad range of services and solutions in strategy, consulting, digital, technology and operations." The company splits its business into five groups: products (27 percent of sales); financial services (20 percent); communications, media, and technology (21 percent); health and public service (17 percent); and resources (15 percent). The company is based in Ireland. Though it currently pays semiannual dividends, the company will move to quarterly dividends in its Fiscal Year 2020, beginning September 2019. The company's dividends are subject to an Irish dividend withholding tax – though investors in certain countries, the U.S. included, may be exempt. Check how the withholding tax applies to you. In September 2018, the company announced a 10 percent increase in its annual dividend to $1.46. As well, also in September 2018, the company committed $5.0 billion to a new share repurchase plan, the $5.0 billion representing about 5 percent of the company's market capitalization.

Here is the checklist and my entries:

1. Does the business make sense?

    a) Stable or falling competition. Yes.

    b) Stable, modestly growing profits. Yes. Earnings per share growth has averaged 12 percent the last 10 years. Earnings growth rate, net of all the accounting distortions, appears reasonably stable.

    c) [Ideally, share counts fall 1-2 percent a year.] Yes, -1.0 percent a year the last 8 years. In aggregate, the number of shares has dropped 8 percent over this period.

    d) Reasonable risks. Probably, though technology does change rapidly. The stock is more volatile than a typical dividend growth stock of the same size. The company faces competition from lower-cost providers, though it does have a big presence, through its Global Delivery Network, in India and the Philippines.

2. Do the financials confirm the story?

    a) [Profit margins are good or strong.] Good, currently, 10 percent. The 10-year average is reasonable, 9 percent.

Year	Sales	Earnings	Assets	Equity	EPS	DPS
2017	34.9	3.4	22.7	9.7	5.91	2.42
2016	32.9	4.1	20.6	8.2	5.34	2.20
2015	31.0	3.1	18.3	6.1	4.82	2.04
2014	30.0	2.9	17.9	5.7	4.52	1.86
2013	28.6	3.3	16.9	5.0	4.21	1.62
2012	27.9	2.6	16.7	4.1	3.84	1.35
2011	25.5	2.3	15.7	3.9	3.39	0.90
2010	21.6	1.8	12.8	2.8	2.66	1.12
2009	21.6	1.6	12.3	2.8	2.44	0.50
2008	23.4	1.7	12.4	2.4	2.64	0.42
2007	19.7	1.2	10.7	2.1	1.97	0.35

Table 6.1: Financial data for Accenture. Numbers are in billions except for EPS (earnings per share) and DPS (dividends per share). Some numbers are adjusted. The company's fiscal year ends in August.

    b) Moderate financial leverage. Yes, 2.3. With regular, recurring revenues, Accenture should have few problems with debt.

    c) *A long-run return on beginning equity average of twenty percent or more.* Yes, the 10-year average is 66 percent. Currently, return on beginning equity is 42 percent.

3. Does the payout ratio signal the right maturity?

    a) A payout ratio that averages at least fifty percent. Yes.

4. Is expected growth reasonable?

    a) A moderate expected five-year earnings per share growth rate. Yes.

5. Never pay too much.

    a) Value the stock correctly. Using a payout ratio of 80 percent and an average growth rate in earnings over the next 30 years of 9.0 percent, at a stock price of $165.00, and earnings per share of $7.00 – implying a current P/E ratio of 24 – the expected return is 11.6 percent a year.

AMPHENOL

Amphenol (ticker: APH) is a stock that many dividend growth funds would miss because of their insistence on *long* records of dividend growth. With Amphenol, it has only been since 2012 that the company started ratcheting up its dividend. Prior to 2012, the company had kept its dividend constant for *seven* years, paying a paltry, token dividend. Prior to that, nothing. I am not as beholden to history. I like the company for its consistently good and stable return on equity and its *remarkably* stable, moderate growth. Think of Amphenol as a play on the ubiquitous growth in electronics but without nearly as much uncertainty, or competition, as many brand-new areas. The company is a global leader in interconnect technology, interconnects being any product that connects one part of a system to another, thus, for instance, electrical and electronic connectors. The company also sells antennas, sensors, and cables. The company serves a broad range of markets. It makes small acquisitions regularly. In April 2018, the company announced a 21 percent increase in its annual dividend to $0.92. Currently, the company has committed to buying back $1.7 billion of its shares, about 6 percent of its market capitalization.

Here is the checklist and my entries:

1. Does the business make sense?

   a) Stable or falling competition. Stable.

   b) Stable, modestly growing profits. Yes. (Adjusted) earnings per share growth has averaged 10 percent a year.

   c) [Ideally, share counts fall 1-2 percent a year.] Yes, -1.5 percent a year the last 10 years. In aggregate, the number of shares has dropped 14 percent over this period.

   d) Reasonable risks. Yes, though, as broadly diversified as the company is, about half of its business comes from the communications industry. Other than that, the major risk is a general economic slowdown.

2. Do the financials confirm the story?

   a) [Profit margins are good or strong.] Good, currently, after an accounting adjustment, 14 percent. The 10-year average is also good, 13 percent.

   b) Moderate financial leverage. Yes, 2.5.

Year	Sales	Earnings	Assets	Equity	EPS	DPS
2017	7011	651	10004	3990	3.12	0.70
2016	6286	823	8499	3675	2.72	0.58
2015	5569	764	7458	3239	2.43	0.53
2014	5346	709	6986	2907	2.25	0.45
2013	4615	636	6150	2860	1.93	0.30
2012	4292	555	5215	2430	1.74	0.21
2011	3940	524	4445	2172	1.52	0.03
2010	3554	496	4016	2321	1.35	0.03
2009	2820	318	3219	1746	0.92	0.03
2008	3236	419	2994	1349	1.17	0.03
2007	2851	353	2676	1265	0.97	0.03

Table 6.2: Financial data for Amphenol. Numbers are in millions except for EPS (earnings per share) and DPS (dividends per share). EPS is adjusted. The company's fiscal year ends in December.

c) *A long-run return on beginning equity average of twenty percent or more.* Yes, the 10-year average is 26 percent. Currently, return on beginning equity, after an accounting adjustment, is also 26 percent.

3. Does the payout ratio signal the right maturity?

   a) A payout ratio that averages at least fifty percent. Currently, perhaps not. I am willing to let this pass. It should comfortably exceed 50 percent soon enough.

4. Is expected growth reasonable?

   a) A moderate expected five-year earnings per share growth rate. Yes.

5. Never pay too much.

   a) Value the stock correctly. Using a payout ratio of 60 percent and an average growth rate in earnings over the next 30 years of 10.0 percent, at a stock price of $92.50, and earnings per share of $3.85 – implying a current P/E ratio of 24 – the expected return is 10.8 percent a year.

ANALOG DEVICES

Analog Devices (ticker: ADI) is a semiconductor company with a primary focus on analog chips. Analog chips are a complement to digital chips, the latter processing information in terms of 1's and 0's (computers do this), while the former processing continuous information like temperature and sound. Since the real world is continuous, you can think of analog chips as processing real-world signals. The company's largest market is the industrial market, about 46 percent of sales. It is well diversified with 125,000 customers. In 2017, it made a sizable acquisition, Linear Technology. The company targets a long-term earnings per share growth rate of 8-12 percent a year. In February 2018, the company announced a 7 percent increase in its annual dividend to $1.92. Currently, the company has committed to buying back $2.0 billion of its shares, about 6 percent of its market capitalization.

Here is the checklist and my entries:

1. Does the business make sense?

    a) Stable or falling competition. Stable.

    b) Stable, modestly growing profits. No. (Adjusted) earnings per share growth has averaged 10 percent a year. (Adjusted) earnings growth rate has not been stable. Earnings are adjusted because of many reasonably large and regular one-time items.

    c) [Ideally, share counts fall 1-2 percent a year.] No, the number of shares has increased 2.0 percent a year the last 10 years. In aggregate, because of the acquisition, the number of shares has risen 21 percent over this period.

    d) Reasonable risks. Perhaps. Apple is a big customer, responsible for 14 percent of company sales. Some of the company's markets are cyclical. Business can be quite volatile.

2. Do the financials confirm the story?

    a) [Profit margins are good or strong.] Good, currently, 14 percent. The 10-year average is strong, 23 percent.

    b) Moderate financial leverage. Close enough, 2.1.

    c) *A long-run return on beginning equity average of twenty percent or more.* Excluding the current year, skewed because of Linear, the prior 9-year average is 20 percent. Currently, return on beginning equity is 14 percent.

Year	Sales	Earnings	Assets	Equity	EPS	DPS
2017	5108	727	21141	10162	4.72	1.77
2016	3421	862	7970	5166	3.07	1.66
2015	3435	697	7059	5073	3.17	1.57
2014	2865	629	6855	4758	2.39	1.45
2013	2664	673	6376	4740	2.14	1.32
2012	2701	651	5620	4165	2.13	1.15
2011	2993	861	5278	3795	2.72	0.94
2010	2762	711	4329	3200	2.33	0.84
2009	2015	248	3404	2529	0.97	0.80
2008	2583	786	3091	2420	1.77	0.76
2007	2430	497	2972	2338	1.48	0.70

Table 6.3: Financial data for Analog Devices. Numbers are in millions except for EPS (earnings per share) and DPS (dividends per share). EPS is (considerably) adjusted to remove one-time effects. The company's fiscal year ends in late October or early November.

3. Does the payout ratio signal the right maturity?

   a) A payout ratio that averages at least fifty percent. Yes.

4. Is expected growth reasonable?

   a) A moderate expected five-year earnings per share growth rate. Yes.

5. Never pay too much.

   a) Value the stock correctly. Using a payout ratio of 70 percent and an average growth rate in earnings over the next 30 years of 9.0 percent, at a stock price of $96.00, and (adjusted) earnings per share of $6.00 – implying a current (adjusted) P/E ratio of 16 – the expected return is 12.8 percent a year. However, volatility can be quite high, leading to lower than expected compounded average returns.

BECTON DICKINSON

Becton Dickinson (ticker: BDX) is a broad-based medical technology company. It operates in two segments, medical and life sciences, with its medical segment about twice as large as its life sciences segment. The company's purpose is to "help the people who help the patients." Because of two transformational acquisitions – CareFusion in March 2015 and C. R. Bard in December 2017 – the company is *considerably* larger than it would have been otherwise. Over the near term, the company expects a higher earnings per share growth rate after the C. R. Bard acquisition – from ten percent a year to the mid-teens. In November 2017, the company announced a 3 percent increase in its annual dividend to $3.00, its 46th consecutive annual increase. Share buybacks are currently muted as the company focuses on paying back debt related to the acquisitions.

Here is the checklist and my entries:

1. Does the business make sense?

    a) Stable or falling competition. Stable.

    b) Stable, modestly growing profits. No. Earnings per share growth has averaged 12 percent the last 10 years. Earnings growth has not been stable.

    c) [Ideally, share counts fall 1-2 percent a year.] No, fair, -0.7 percent a year the last 10 years. In aggregate, the number of shares has dropped 7 percent over this period. (The company issued shares as part of the cost of the acquisitions.)

    d) Reasonable risks. Yes.

2. Do the financials confirm the story?

    a) [Profit margins are good or strong.] Reasonable, currently, 9 percent, though this reflects accounting adjustments, which serve, in this case, to bring the profit margin down. The 10-year average is good, 14 percent.

    b) Moderate financial leverage. Perhaps a bit high, 2.9. The company's current focus is to pay down the debt related to the acquisitions.

    c) *A long-run return on beginning equity average of twenty percent or more.* Yes, the 10-year average is 22 percent. Currently, return on beginning equity is 14 percent, reflecting recent acquisition-related accounting adjustments.

Year	Sales	Earnings	Assets	Equity	EPS	DPS
2017	12093	1100	37734	12948	9.48	2.92
2016	12483	976	25586	7633	8.59	2.64
2015	10282	695	26478	7164	7.16	2.40
2014	8446	1185	12447	5053	6.50	2.18
2013	8054	1293	12149	5043	6.07	1.98
2012	7708	1170	11361	4136	5.30	1.80
2011	7584	1271	10430	4828	5.31	1.64
2010	7124	1318	9651	5435	4.64	1.48
2009	6987	1232	9305	5143	4.73	1.32
2008	6898	1127	7913	4936	4.27	1.14
2007	6121	890	7329	4362	3.20	0.98

Table 6.4: Financial data for Becton-Dickinson. Numbers are in millions except for EPS (earnings per share) and DPS (dividends per share). Some numbers are adjusted. The company's fiscal year ends in September.

3. Does the payout ratio signal the right maturity?

   a) A payout ratio that averages at least fifty percent. Yes, but with a focus on paying down debt, for now, the payout ratio is temporarily subdued.

4. Is expected growth reasonable?

   a) A moderate expected five-year earnings per share growth rate. No, but in a good way – earnings per share should grow about 14 percent a year the next five years.

5. Never pay too much.

   a) Value the stock correctly. Using a payout ratio of 60 percent and an average growth rate in earnings over the next 30 years of 9.0 percent, at a stock price of $250.00, and earnings per share of $11.50 – implying a current P/E ratio of 22 – the expected return is 10.4 percent a year.

BROWN-FORMAN

Brown-Forman (ticker: BF-B) was founded in 1870 and is still run as a family-controlled business. It sells premium spirits, in particular whiskeys, the key brand being Jack Daniel's. Some of its many other brands include Finlandia, Korbel, el Jimador, Woodford Reserve, and Old Forrester. The company has been listed since 1934 and has paid dividends for 73 consecutive years. Brown-Forman has two classes of stock, A, with voting privileges, and controlled by the Brown family, and B, without voting privileges. Class B is what I refer to here. In November 2017, the company announced an 8 percent increase in its annual dividend to $0.632, its 34th consecutive annual increase. (The odd-looking $0.632 reflects a subsequent 5-for-4 stock split in 2018.) Currently, the company has committed to buying back $0.2 billion of its shares, about 1 percent of its market capitalization.

Here is the checklist and my entries:

1. Does the business make sense?

    a) Stable or falling competition. Maybe. There are many big players in the industry and plenty of new brands coming out regularly as well. That said, the company has a stable of strong brands.

    b) Stable, modestly growing profits. Yes. Earnings per share growth has averaged 10 percent the last 10 years.

    c) [Ideally, share counts fall 1-2 percent a year.] Yes, -1.6 percent a year the last 10 years. In aggregate, the number of shares has dropped 15 percent over this period.

    d) Reasonable risks. Yes, though, of course, consumer tastes can change. Still, it is hard to imagine that Jack Daniel's, for instance, is going to go out of style any time soon.

2. Do the financials confirm the story?

    a) [Profit margins are good or strong.] Strong, currently, 22 percent. The 10-year average is also strong, 22 percent.

    b) Moderate financial leverage. Perhaps. Financial leverage of 3.8 seems high, though, as with many of our dividend growth stocks, the business is recurring.

    c) *A long-run return on beginning equity average of twenty percent or more.* Yes, the 10-year average is 36 percent. Currently, return on beginning equity is 52 percent.

Year	Sales	Earnings	Assets	Equity	EPS	DPS
2018	3248	717	4976	1316	1.48	1.61
2017	2994	669	4625	1370	1.37	0.56
2016	3089	1067	4183	1562	2.09	0.52
2015	3134	684	4188	1900	1.28	0.48
2014	2991	659	4103	2032	1.22	0.44
2013	2849	591	3626	1628	1.10	1.99
2012	2723	513	3477	2069	0.95	0.36
2011	2586	572	3712	2060	1.04	0.60
2010	2469	449	3383	1895	0.81	0.31
2009	2481	435	3475	1816	0.77	0.30
2008	2582	440	3405	1725	0.76	0.27

Table 6.5: Financial data for Brown-Forman. Numbers are in millions except for EPS (earnings per share) and DPS (dividends per share). EPS and DPS reflect multiple stock splits. DPS includes one-time dividends. The company's fiscal year ends in April.

3. Does the payout ratio signal the right maturity?

   a) A payout ratio that averages at least fifty percent. Yes.

4. Is expected growth reasonable?

   a) A moderate expected five-year earnings per share growth rate. Yes.

5. Never pay too much.

   a) Value the stock correctly. Using a payout ratio of 80 percent and an average growth rate in earnings over the next 30 years of 8.0 percent, at a stock price of $52.50, and earnings per share of $1.70 – implying a current P/E ratio of 31 – the expected return is 9.3 percent a year. This P/E ratio is well outside the range of our magic formula so I used the spreadsheet from my book, *Investing in Dividend Growth Stocks*, to check. The spreadsheet yielded – reassuringly – 9.2 percent a year.

Church & Dwight

Church & Dwight (ticker: CHD) is the company behind ARM & HAMMER, Trojan, OxiClean, more than 80 consumer brands in all. Eleven of its brands generate more than 80 percent of sales. Because the company sells a mix of premium (65 percent of its business) and value brands (35 percent), it believes it will generally do well in most economic environments. Acquisitions are a vital part of its strategy – the company considers itself a "serial acquirer." The company targets a long-term earnings per share growth rate of 8 percent a year. In February 2018, the company announced a 14 percent increase in its annual dividend to $0.87. Remarkably, the company has paid regular quarterly dividends for 117 years. Currently, the company has committed to buying back $0.31 billion of its shares, about 2 percent of its market capitalization. The company does not pass some of our tests, but is interesting nonetheless as a company that prioritizes acquisitions over share buybacks. It is difficult to value.

Here is the checklist and my entries:

1. Does the business make sense?

   a) Stable or falling competition. Stable.

   b) Stable, modestly growing profits. Yes. Earnings per share growth has averaged 12 percent the last 10 years. Earnings growth rate has been "reasonably" stable.

   c) [Ideally, share counts fall 1-2 percent a year.] No, fair, -0.8 percent a year the last 10 years. In aggregate, the number of shares has dropped 8 percent over this period.

   d) Reasonable risks. Yes, though one customer, Wal-Mart, accounts for 24 percent of sales.

2. Do the financials confirm the story?

   a) [Profit margins are good or strong.] Good, currently, 13 percent. The 10-year average is also good, 11 percent.

   b) Moderate financial leverage. Maybe, 2.7.

   c) *A long-run return on beginning equity average of twenty percent or more.* No, the 10-year average is 19 percent, though with the recent tax cut, and company trends, the 10-year average should soon get there. Currently, return on beginning equity is 25 percent.

Year	Sales	Earnings	Assets	Equity	EPS	DPS
2017	3776	498	6015	2218	1.94	0.76
2016	3493	464	4354	1978	1.77	0.71
2015	3395	410	4257	2023	1.62	0.67
2014	3298	414	4359	2102	1.51	0.62
2013	3194	394	4237	2300	1.40	0.56
2012	2922	350	4072	2061	1.23	0.48
2011	2749	310	3105	2041	1.06	0.34
2010	2589	271	2945	1871	0.94	0.16
2009	2521	244	3118	1602	0.85	0.12
2008	2422	195	2801	1332	0.69	0.09
2007	2221	169	2533	1081	0.61	0.07

Table 6.6: Financial data for Church & Dwight. Numbers are in millions except for EPS (earnings per share) and DPS (dividends per share). Some numbers are adjusted. The company's fiscal year ends in December.

3. Does the payout ratio signal the right maturity?

   a) A payout ratio that averages at least fifty percent. Maybe, and even then not by a large margin as the company spends a lot on acquisitions, its priority.

4. Is expected growth reasonable?

   a) A moderate expected five-year earnings per share growth rate. Yes.

5. Never pay too much.

   a) Value the stock correctly. Using a payout ratio of 55 percent and an average growth rate in earnings over the next 30 years of 7.0 percent, at a stock price of $53.00, and earnings per share of $2.25 – implying a current P/E ratio of 24 – the expected return is 7.8 percent a year, though I suspect the company will do better. Acquisitive companies are tricky to value correctly. Think of this as a fair minimum.

COSTCO

Costco (ticker: COST) is the train that keeps on chugging. Even though it is the second largest retailer in the world, it has ample room to grow globally. Of its 749 warehouses, 519 are located in the U.S., with others in Canada, Mexico, the U.K., Japan, Korea, Taiwan, Australia, Spain, Ireland, and France. Customers pay a membership fee in exchange for excellent prices. The business model is simplicity itself: Let gross margins cover internal company expenses, thus ensuring – as long as there is not much organizational bloat – the lowest possible prices. Essentially, shareholders "keep" the after-tax portion of membership fees plus whatever the company chooses to pass on to shareholders from productivity gains. That's about as good a business model as you will find. Costco has paid some *huge* one-time dividends recently, though these have been offset, effectively, by a relatively stagnant share count over the last ten years and increased debt. In April 2018, the company announced a 14 percent increase in its annual dividend to $2.28. Currently, the company has committed to buying back 2.5 million of its shares, about 2 percent of its shares outstanding.

Here is the checklist and my entries:

1. Does the business make sense?

   a) Stable or falling competition. Yes.

   b) Stable, modestly growing profits. Yes. Earnings per share growth has averaged 10 percent the last 10 years. Earnings growth rate has been stable.

   c) [Ideally, share counts fall 1-2 percent a year.] No, the number of shares has actually remained roughly constant over the last ten years.

   d) Reasonable risks. Yes.

2. Do the financials confirm the story?

   a) [Profit margins are good or strong.] Low, currently, 2 percent. The 10-year average is also low, 2 percent. This is in the nature of Costco's business model.

   b) Moderate financial leverage. No, 3.4, though not an issue for Costco with its regular, recurring business.

   c) *A long-run return on beginning equity average of twenty percent or more.* Close, the 10-year average is 17 percent. Currently, return on beginning equity is 22 percent.

Year	Sales	Earnings	Assets	Equity	EPS	DPS
2017	129.0	2.7	36.3	10.8	6.08	8.90
2016	118.7	2.4	33.2	12.1	5.33	1.70
2015	116.2	2.4	33.4	10.6	5.37	6.51
2014	112.6	2.1	33.0	12.3	4.65	1.33
2013	105.2	2.0	30.3	10.8	4.63	8.17
2012	99.1	1.7	27.1	12.4	3.89	1.03
2011	88.9	1.5	26.8	12.0	3.30	0.89
2010	77.9	1.3	23.8	10.8	2.92	0.77
2009	71.4	1.1	22.0	10.0	2.47	0.68
2008	72.5	1.3	20.7	9.2	2.89	0.61
2007	64.4	1.1	19.6	8.6	2.37	0.55

Table 6.7: Financial data for Costco. Numbers are in billions except for EPS (earnings per share) and DPS (dividends per share). The company paid sizable one-time dividends in 2013 ($7), 2015 ($5), and 2017 ($7). The company's fiscal year ends in late August or early September.

3. Does the payout ratio signal the right maturity?

   a) A payout ratio that averages at least fifty percent. Yes.

4. Is expected growth reasonable?

   a) A moderate expected five-year earnings per share growth rate. Yes.

5. Never pay too much.

   a) Value the stock correctly. Using a payout ratio of 75 percent and an average growth rate in earnings over the next 30 years of 10.0 percent, at a stock price of $230.00, and earnings per share of $7.30 – implying a current P/E ratio of 32 – the expected return is 10.5 percent a year. This P/E ratio is well outside the range of our magic formula so I used the spreadsheet from my book, *Investing in Dividend Growth Stocks*, to confirm. It – reassuringly – yielded 10.4 percent a year.

GRACO

Graco (ticker: GGG) is a global leader in fluid handling. It makes premium equipment to move, measure, control, dispense, and spray fluid and coating materials. The company splits its business into three segments: industrial (47 percent of sales); contractor (33 percent); and process (20 percent). The company's largest end market is construction, with construction typically responsible for more than 40 percent of company sales. Acquisitions are an important part of the company's strategy. Graco has a continuous improvement culture and has been a strong and consistent performer over long periods. The company's goal is to grow earnings per share 12 percent a year, compounded. In December 2017, the company announced a 10 percent increase in its annual dividend to $0.53. Currently, the company has committed to buying back 5.3 million of its shares, about 3 percent of its shares outstanding.

Here is the checklist and my entries:

1. Does the business make sense?

   a) Stable or falling competition. Yes.

   b) Stable, modestly growing profits. No. Earnings per share growth has averaged 15 percent the last 10 years. Earnings growth rate has not been stable.

   c) [Ideally, share counts fall 1-2 percent a year.] Yes, -1.0 percent a year the last 10 years. In aggregate, the number of shares has dropped 10 percent over this period.

   d) Reasonable risks. Yes, though the company does depend on cyclical industries where activity can decline sharply during economic downturns.

2. Do the financials confirm the story?

   a) [Profit margins are good or strong.] Strong, currently, 17 percent. The 10-year average is good, 15 percent.

   b) Moderate financial leverage. Yes, 1.9.

   c) *A long-run return on beginning equity average of twenty percent or more.* Yes, the 10-year average is 42 percent. Currently, return on beginning equity is 44 percent.

3. Does the payout ratio signal the right maturity?

Year	Sales	Earnings	Assets	Equity	EPS	DPS
2017	1475	252	1379	723	4.35	1.47
2016	1329	202	1243	574	3.55	1.35
2015	1286	205	1391	636	3.46	1.20
2014	1221	226	1545	596	3.23	1.10
2013	1104	211	1327	634	3.36	1.00
2012	1012	149	1322	454	2.42	0.90
2011	895	142	874	323	2.32	0.84
2010	744	103	530	264	1.69	0.80
2009	579	49	476	210	0.81	0.76
2008	817	121	580	168	1.99	0.74
2007	841	153	537	245	2.32	0.66

Table 6.8: Financial data for Graco. Numbers are in millions except for EPS (earnings per share) and DPS (dividends per share). Some numbers are adjusted. The company's fiscal year ends in December.

    a) A payout ratio that averages at least fifty percent. Yes.

4. Is expected growth reasonable?

    a) A moderate expected five-year earnings per share growth rate. Yes.

5. Never pay too much.

    a) Value the stock correctly. Using a payout ratio of 65 percent and an average growth rate in earnings over the next 30 years of 11.0 percent, at a stock price of $45.00, and earnings per share of $1.85 – implying a current P/E ratio of 24 – the expected return is 12.1 percent a year.

ILLINOIS TOOL WORKS

Illinois Tool Works (ticker: ITW) makes a broad range of industrial products for a wide variety of markets: automotive OEM, test and measurement and electronics, food equipment, polymers and fluids, welding, and construction. In addition, it runs a specialty products segment. Per the company, "[its] seven industry-leading segments leverage the unique ITW Business Model to drive solid growth with best-in-class margins and returns in markets where highly innovative, customer-focused solutions are required." In August 2018, the company announced a 28 percent increase in its annual dividend to $4.00. The company has increased its dividend for more than 55 consecutive years, "except during a period of government controls in 1971." Currently, the company has committed to buying back $4.4 billion of its shares, about 9 percent of its market capitalization.

Here is the checklist and my entries:

1. Does the business make sense?

   a) Stable or falling competition. Stable.

   b) Stable, modestly growing profits. No. Earnings per share growth has averaged 7 percent the last 10 years. Earnings growth rate has not been stable.

   c) [Ideally, share counts fall 1-2 percent a year.] Even better, exceptional, -4.2 percent a year the last 10 years, though it appears that these buybacks were accompanied by a sizable increase in debt. Thus, as positive as it is, it is not quite the same as buying back the shares with cash generated by the business. To be fair, many companies have done the same – to take advantage of low interest rates. As long as debt is not excessive, it is the right thing to do. In aggregate, the number of shares has dropped 35 percent over this period.

   d) Reasonable risks. Yes. With its broad range of products and markets, general economic slowdowns are probably its greatest risk, though in the grand scheme of things, this is a risk faced by almost every company.

2. Do the financials confirm the story?

   a) [Profit margins are good or strong.] Good, currently, 12 percent. The 10-year average is also good, 13 percent.

Year	Sales	Earnings	Assets	Equity	EPS	DPS
2017	14.3	1.7	16.8	4.6	4.86	2.86
2016	13.6	2.0	15.2	4.3	5.70	2.40
2015	13.4	1.9	15.7	5.2	5.13	2.07
2014	14.5	2.9	17.5	6.8	4.67	1.81
2013	14.1	1.7	20.0	9.7	3.63	1.60
2012	14.8	2.9	19.3	10.6	4.72	1.48
2011	14.5	2.1	18.0	10.0	4.19	1.40
2010	15.4	1.5	16.4	9.6	2.99	1.30
2009	13.6	1.0	16.1	8.8	1.94	1.24
2008	17.1	1.5	15.2	7.7	2.91	1.18
2007	16.1	1.9	15.5	9.4	3.36	0.98

Table 6.9: Financial data for Illinois Tool Works. Numbers are in billions except for EPS (earnings per share) and DPS (dividends per share). The company's fiscal year ends in December.

    b) Moderate financial leverage. No, excessive, 3.7.

    c) *A long-run return on beginning equity average of twenty percent or more.* Yes, the 10-year average is 25 percent. Currently, return on beginning equity is 40 percent.

3. Does the payout ratio signal the right maturity?

    a) A payout ratio that averages at least fifty percent. Yes.

4. Is expected growth reasonable?

    a) A moderate expected five-year earnings per share growth rate. Yes, though the company may exceed our 12-percent maximum over this period. No-one's complaining if they do.

5. Never pay too much.

    a) Value the stock correctly. Using a payout ratio of 75 percent and an average growth rate in earnings over the next 30 years of 6.0 percent, at a stock price of $140.00, and earnings per share of $7.60 – implying a current P/E ratio of 18 – the expected return is 9.7 percent a year.

MCCORMICK

McCormick (ticker: MKC) makes, markets, and distributes spices and other flavor-related products. The company operates in two segments, consumer (62 percent of sales) and industrial (38 percent). The consumer segment is the more profitable of the two. In the industrial segment, the company's customers are food manufacturers and food-service companies. Acquisitions are an important part of the company's strategy. The company's long-term goal is to increase earnings per share 9-11 percent a year. In November 2017, the company announced an 11 percent increase in its annual dividend to $2.08, its 32nd consecutive annual increase. To reduce the debt incurred with a recent sizable acquisition, the company has decided to curtail its share buybacks for the time being. It has a relatively small amount, $140 million (equivalent to less than a percent of its market capitalization), left on its current share repurchase authorization.

Here is the checklist and my entries:

1. Does the business make sense?

    a) Stable or falling competition. Maybe. Private labels are a constant threat though the company, itself, participates in the private-label market.

    b) Stable, modestly growing profits. No. Earnings per share growth has averaged 8 percent the last 10 years. Earnings growth rate has not been stable.

    c) [Ideally, share counts fall 1-2 percent a year.] No, the number of shares has actually increased 0.3 percent a year the last 10 years. In aggregate, the number of shares has risen 3 percent over this period.

    d) Reasonable risks. Yes. Consumers pay up for its brand name. Any damage to its brand name will hurt its sales.

2. Do the financials confirm the story?

    a) [Profit margins are good or strong.] Good, currently, 10 percent. The 10-year average is also good, 10 percent.

    b) Moderate financial leverage. No, excessive, 4.0, a consequence of the recent sizable acquisition.

    c) *A long-run return on beginning equity average of twenty percent or more.* Yes, the 10-year average is 25 percent. Currently, return on beginning equity is 29 percent.

Year	Sales	Earnings	Assets	Equity	EPS	DPS
2017	4834	477	10386	2571	3.72	1.93
2016	4412	472	4636	1638	3.69	1.76
2015	4296	402	4508	1687	3.11	1.63
2014	4243	438	4414	1809	3.34	1.51
2013	4123	389	4450	1948	2.91	1.39
2012	4014	408	4165	1700	3.04	1.27
2011	3698	374	4088	1619	2.79	1.15
2010	3337	370	3420	1463	2.75	1.06
2009	3192	300	3388	1344	2.27	0.98
2008	3177	256	3220	1063	1.94	0.90
2007	2916	230	2788	1095	1.73	0.82

Table 6.10: Financial data for McCormick. Numbers are in millions except for EPS (earnings per share) and DPS (dividends per share). The company's fiscal year ends in November.

3. Does the payout ratio signal the right maturity?

   a) A payout ratio that averages at least fifty percent. Yes, on average, though the company sometimes reduces its share buybacks considerably. It did so during the Crash of 2008. It is doing so now. The company places an emphasis on acquisitions.

4. Is expected growth reasonable?

   a) A moderate expected five-year earnings per share growth rate. Yes.

5. Never pay too much.

   a) Value the stock correctly. Using a payout ratio of 60 percent and an average growth rate in earnings over the next 30 years of 8.0 percent, at a stock price of $120.00, and earnings per share of $5.10 – implying a current P/E ratio of 24 – the expected return is 9.1 percent a year.

McDonald's

McDonald's (ticker: MCD) franchises and operates more than 36,000 McDonald's restaurants in more than 100 countries. The majority – more than 90 percent – of the company's restaurants are franchised. After a difficult few years, the company hired a new CEO in 2015. It has since been doing much better. The company targets long-term sales growth of 3-5 percent a year with earnings per share growth in the high single digits. It is very shareholder-friendly. In September 2018, the company announced a 15 percent increase in its annual dividend to $4.64, its 42nd consecutive annual increase. Currently, the company has committed to buying back $8.9 billion of its shares, about 7 percent of its market capitalization.

Here is the checklist and my entries:

1. Does the business make sense?

    a) Stable or falling competition. No. The fast-food business is a competitive nightmare.

    b) Stable, modestly growing profits. No. Earnings per share growth has averaged 6 percent the last 9 years. The earnings growth rate has been stable over this period.

    c) [Ideally, share counts fall 1-2 percent a year.] Even better, exceptional, -3.6 percent a year the last 10 years. In aggregate, the number of shares has dropped 31 percent over this period.

    d) Reasonable risks. Perhaps. While the fast-food business is intensely competitive, the company has the benefit of (vast) scale.

2. Do the financials confirm the story?

    a) [Profit margins are good or strong.] Strong, currently, 23 percent. The 10-year average is also strong, 20 percent. Both are a reflection of the company acting primarily as a franchisor.

    b) Moderate financial leverage. The company has negative equity. While this would not be a good development for an individual, for a company with strong recurring revenues it is not a big deal. In fact, this kind of financial engineering often benefits shareholders in a big way.

Year	Sales	Earnings	Assets	Equity	EPS	DPS
2017	22.8	5.2	33.8	-3.3	6.37	3.83
2016	24.6	4.7	31.0	-2.2	5.44	3.61
2015	25.4	4.5	37.9	7.1	4.80	3.44
2014	27.4	4.8	34.3	12.9	4.82	3.28
2013	28.1	5.6	36.6	16.0	5.55	3.12
2012	27.6	5.5	35.4	15.3	5.36	2.87
2011	27.0	5.5	33.0	14.4	5.27	2.53
2010	24.0	4.9	32.0	14.6	4.58	2.26
2009	22.7	4.6	30.2	14.0	4.11	2.05
2008	23.5	4.3	28.5	13.4	3.76	1.63
2007	22.8	2.4	29.4	15.3	1.98	1.50

Table 6.11: Financial data for McDonald's. Numbers are in billions except for EPS (earnings per share) and DPS (dividends per share). The company's fiscal year ends in December.

c) *A long-run return on beginning equity average of twenty percent or more.* Not applicable, as the company has negative equity. Ignoring the last two years, over the prior eight, the return on beginning equity was 34 percent.

3. Does the payout ratio signal the right maturity?

a) A payout ratio that averages at least fifty percent. Yes.

4. Is expected growth reasonable?

a) A moderate expected five-year earnings per share growth rate. Yes.

5. Never pay too much.

a) Value the stock correctly. Using a payout ratio of 85 percent and an average growth rate in earnings over the next 30 years of 5.0 percent, at a stock price of $160.00, and earnings per share of $7.75 – implying a current P/E ratio of 21 – the expected return is 9.0 percent a year.

NIKE

Nike (ticker: NKE) designs and sells athletic footwear, clothing, equipment, accessories, and services. The company is the largest seller of athletic footwear and clothing in the world. Its key brands are NIKE and Jordan. It also owns Converse and Hurley. Nike considers itself a growth company. In fact, putting aside the company's Fiscal Year 2018 results, Nike's earnings per share growth rate of 14 percent over the previous nine years exceeds our moderate growth requirement for large companies of 8-12 percent. In November 2017, the company announced an 11 percent increase in its annual dividend to $0.80, its 16th consecutive annual increase. Currently, the company has committed to buying back $3.3 billion of its shares, about 2 percent of its market capitalization.

Here is the checklist and my entries:

1. Does the business make sense?

    a) Stable or falling competition. Perhaps. Adidas is gaining more than a foothold, so to speak, in the U.S., though after a tricky couple of years, Nike seems to be fighting back successfully.

    b) Stable, modestly growing profits. No, but in a good way – ignoring the most recent year, earnings per share growth averaged 14 percent the previous 9 years, higher than our maximum of 12 percent. Earnings growth rate has been stable.

    c) [Ideally, share counts fall 1-2 percent a year.] Slightly better, -2.1 percent a year the last 10 years. In aggregate, the number of shares (I consider only Nike's Class B shares) has dropped 19 percent over this period.

    d) Reasonable risks. Yes, though increasing competition from Adidas and the like, if it does come to pass, is never a good thing. Consumer tastes can be fickle. Any damage to its brand will hurt its sales. Still, Nike is Nike and you'd expect them to prevail over the long term. This company knows how to market and sell.

2. Do the financials confirm the story?

    a) [Profit margins are good or strong.] Reasonable, currently, 5 percent. The 10-year average is good, 10 percent.

Year	Sales	Earnings	Assets	Equity	EPS	DPS
2018	36.4	1.9	22.5	9.8	1.17	0.78
2017	34.4	4.2	23.3	12.4	2.51	0.70
2016	32.4	3.8	21.4	12.3	2.16	0.62
2015	30.6	3.3	21.6	12.7	1.85	0.54
2014	27.8	2.7	18.6	10.8	1.49	0.47
2013	25.3	2.5	17.6	11.1	1.35	0.41
2012	23.3	2.2	15.5	10.4	1.19	0.35
2011	20.9	2.1	15.0	9.8	1.10	0.30
2010	19.0	1.9	14.4	9.8	0.96	0.27
2009	19.2	1.5	13.2	8.7	0.76	0.24
2008	18.6	1.9	12.4	7.8	0.94	0.22

Table 6.12: Financial data for Nike. Numbers are in billions except for EPS (earnings per share) and DPS (dividends per share). The company's fiscal year ends in May.

    b) Moderate financial leverage. Maybe, 2.3.

    c) *A long-run return on beginning equity average of twenty percent or more.* Yes, the 10-year average is 24 percent. Currently, return on beginning equity is 15 percent.

3. Does the payout ratio signal the right maturity?

    a) A payout ratio that averages at least fifty percent. Yes.

4. Is expected growth reasonable?

    a) A moderate expected five-year earnings per share growth rate. Yes.

5. Never pay too much.

    a) Value the stock correctly. Using a payout ratio of 70 percent and an average growth rate in earnings over the next 30 years of 9.0 percent, at a stock price of $80.00, and earnings per share of $2.70 – implying a current P/E ratio of 30, and slightly higher than the validity of our magic formula, which I choose to ignore – the expected return is 9.7 percent a year.

PACCAR

Paccar (ticker: PCAR) designs and makes premium trucks under the Kenworth, Peterbilt, and DAF nameplates. It also makes and sells diesel engines and parts, and operates a financial services division and an industrial winches division. Its products are noted for their high quality. Paccar has enjoyed a string of 79 consecutive years of net profits and has paid a dividend every year since 1941. It typically pays a special dividend every year, though it did not pay one in 2009. These special dividends make the pattern of dividends per share look quirky. In May 2018, the company announced a 12 percent increase in its annual dividend to $1.12. Share buybacks are typically quite small. Business can be quite volatile, unlike that of the typical dividend growth stock. In some ways, Paccar barely meets the qualifications of this book but, in my opinion, it is an excellent (operational) company – and worth a look.

Here is the checklist and my entries:

1. Does the business make sense?

   a) Stable or falling competition. Probably. The company continues to gain market share.

   b) Stable, modestly growing profits. No, a function of its markets. Earnings growth rate has not been stable.

   c) [Ideally, share counts fall 1-2 percent a year.] No, fair, -0.4 percent a year the last 10 years. In aggregate, the number of shares has dropped 4 percent over this period. Share buybacks are not a priority. The company prefers dividends.

   d) Reasonable risks. Yes, when averaged over the long term. However, because these are expensive vehicles, demand declines sharply during recessions, earnings collapsing.

2. Do the financials confirm the story?

   a) [Profit margins are good or strong.] Reasonable, currently, 8 percent. The 10-year average is low, 6 percent.

   b) Moderate financial leverage. Yes, 1.3, though this calculation excludes assets of the financial services division.

   c) *A long-run return on beginning equity average of twenty percent or more.* Close, the 10-year average is 18 percent. Currently, return on beginning equity is 22 percent.

Year	Sales	Earnings	Assets	Equity	EPS	DPS
2017	19.5	1.5	10.2	8.1	4.26	2.19
2016	17.0	1.4	8.4	6.8	3.85	1.56
2015	19.1	1.6	8.9	6.9	4.51	2.32
2014	19.0	1.4	8.7	6.8	3.82	1.86
2013	17.1	1.2	9.1	6.6	3.30	1.70
2012	17.1	1.1	7.8	5.8	3.12	1.58
2011	16.4	1.0	7.8	5.4	2.86	1.30
2010	10.3	0.5	6.4	5.4	1.25	0.69
2009	8.1	0.1	6.1	5.1	0.31	0.54
2008	15.0	1.0	6.2	4.8	2.78	0.82
2007	15.2	1.2	6.6	5.0	3.29	1.65

Table 6.13: Financial data for Paccar. Numbers are in billions except for EPS (earnings per share) and DPS (dividends per share). Assets exclude those of the financial division. Earnings and EPS for some years are adjusted. Special dividends are included in dividends per share. The company's fiscal year ends in December.

3. Does the payout ratio signal the right maturity?

   a) A payout ratio that averages at least fifty percent. Just barely, perhaps, when increases in debt are carefully accounted for. The company needs to make heavy investments regularly, reducing what it can pay out to shareholders.

4. Is expected growth reasonable?

   a) A moderate expected five-year earnings per share growth rate. No. According to analysts, the expected earnings per share growth rate is 5 percent.

5. Never pay too much.

   a) Value the stock correctly. Using a payout ratio of 55 percent and an average growth rate in earnings over the next 30 years of 7.0 percent, at a stock price of $60.00, and earnings per share of $6.00 – implying a current P/E ratio of 10 – the expected return is 13.1 percent a year. This feels too high. The market discounts more volatile businesses with lower P/E ratios.

PARKER-HANNIFIN

Parker-Hannifin (ticker: PH) is the global leader in motion and control technologies. The company's tagline is, "Solving the world's greatest engineering challenges." The company makes the gizmos that enable motion and the controlled flow of liquids and gases. Acquisitions are an important part of the company's strategy. The business is well diversified. Over the next five years, the company targets a compound average earnings per share growth rate of at least 10 percent a year. In April 2018, the company announced a 15 percent increase in its annual dividend to $3.04, its 62nd consecutive annual increase. The company raises its dividend, or keeps it flat, on its own schedule. Currently, the company has committed to buying back $16.5 billion of its shares, about 12 percent of its market capitalization. This is an open-ended share buyback program, one with no expiration date.

Here is the checklist and my entries:

1. Does the business make sense?

    a) Stable or falling competition. Probably. The company is the biggest player in a fairly fragmented market though, as evidenced by the company's profit margin, there are sizable competitive players that likely provide ample competition.

    b) Stable, modestly growing profits. No. Earnings per share growth has averaged 8 percent the last 10 years. Earnings growth rate has not been stable.

    c) [Ideally, share counts fall 1-2 percent a year.] Even better, exceptional, -2.3 percent a year the last 10 years. In aggregate, the number of shares has dropped 21 percent over this period.

    d) Reasonable risks. Maybe. Parker is more economically sensitive than a typical dividend growth stock of the same size.

2. Do the financials confirm the story?

    a) [Profit margins are good or strong.] Reasonable, currently, 7 percent. The 10-year average is also reasonable, 7 percent.

    b) Moderate financial leverage. Maybe, 2.6. The company's intention is to reduce debt, as it probably should as this level of debt does look a tad high – in relation to the many cyclical markets that Parker serves.

Year	Sales	Earnings	Assets	Equity	EPS	DPS
2018	14.30	1.06	15.32	5.87	7.83	2.74
2017	12.03	0.98	15.49	5.27	7.25	2.58
2016	11.36	0.81	12.06	4.58	5.89	2.52
2015	12.71	1.01	12.29	5.11	6.97	2.37
2014	13.22	1.04	13.27	6.66	6.87	1.86
2013	13.02	0.95	12.54	5.74	6.26	1.70
2012	13.15	1.15	11.17	4.90	7.45	1.54
2011	12.35	1.05	10.89	5.38	6.37	1.25
2010	9.99	0.55	9.91	4.37	3.40	1.01
2009	10.31	0.51	9.86	4.27	3.13	1.00
2008	12.15	0.95	10.39	5.25	5.53	0.84

Table 6.14: Financial data for Parker-Hannifin. Numbers are in billions except for EPS (earnings per share) and DPS (dividends per share). The company's fiscal year ends in June.

c) *A long-run return on beginning equity average of twenty percent or more.* Close, the 10-year average is 18 percent. Currently, return on beginning equity is 20 percent.

3. Does the payout ratio signal the right maturity?

a) A payout ratio that averages at least fifty percent. Yes.

4. Is expected growth reasonable?

a) A moderate expected five-year earnings per share growth rate. Yes.

5. Never pay too much.

a) Value the stock correctly. Using a payout ratio of 55 percent and an average growth rate in earnings over the next 30 years of 7.0 percent, at a stock price of $175.00, and earnings per share of $10.00 – implying a current P/E ratio of 18 – the expected return is 9.3 percent a year.

ROSS STORES

Ross Stores (ticker: ROST) operates 1,453 Ross Dress for Less stores and 227 dd's DISCOUNTS stores. Ross Dress for Less is the largest off-price apparel and home fashion chain in the U.S. with stores primarily located in middle-class markets. Ross Dress for Less targets discounts of 20 percent to 60 percent off department store and specialty store regular prices. dd's DISCOUNTS offers lower price points and caters to a younger and lower-income demographic. dd's DISCOUNTS targets discounts of 20 percent to 70 percent off moderate department store and discount store regular prices. Long term, the company projects it can grow to 3,000 locations. The company is an aggressive buyer of its shares. In March 2018, the company announced a 41 (stunning!) percent increase in its annual dividend to $0.90, its 24th consecutive annual increase. Currently, the company has committed to buying back $1.6 billion of its shares, about 4 percent of its market capitalization. The company typically announces a target amount to spend on shares each year, spends that amount, then ups the amount the following year. Here is the checklist and my entries:

1. Does the business make sense?

    a) Stable or falling competition. Perhaps. Many retailers are now chasing the off-price concept. Nevertheless, Ross has established a particulary strong niche.

    b) Stable, modestly growing profits. No – but in an extremely good way. Earnings per share growth has averaged 23 percent the last 10 years. Earnings growth rate has been stable.

    c) [Ideally, share counts fall 1-2 percent a year.] Even better, exceptional, -3.4 percent a year the last 10 years. In aggregate, the number of shares has dropped 29 percent over this period.

    d) Reasonable risks. Yes.

2. Do the financials confirm the story?

    a) [Profit margins are good or strong.] Good, currently, 10 percent. The 10-year average is reasonable, 8 percent.

    b) Moderate financial leverage. Yes, 1.9.

    c) *A long-run return on beginning equity average of twenty percent or more.* Yes, the 10-year average is 46 percent. Currently, return on beginning equity is 50 percent.

Year	Sales	Earnings	Assets	Equity	EPS	DPS
2017	14.1	1.4	5.7	3.0	3.55	0.64
2016	12.9	1.1	5.3	2.7	2.83	0.54
2015	11.9	1.0	4.9	2.5	2.51	0.47
2014	11.0	0.9	4.7	2.3	2.21	0.40
2013	10.2	0.8	3.9	2.0	1.94	0.34
2012	9.7	0.8	3.7	1.8	1.76	0.28
2011	8.6	0.7	3.3	1.5	1.43	0.22
2010	7.9	0.6	3.1	1.3	1.16	0.16
2009	7.2	0.4	2.8	1.2	0.89	0.11
2008	6.8	0.3	2.4	1.0	0.58	0.10
2007	6.0	0.3	2.4	1.0	0.48	0.08

Table 6.15: Financial data for Ross Stores. Numbers are in billions except for EPS (earnings per share) and DPS (dividends per share). The company's fiscal year ends in late January or early February.

3. Does the payout ratio signal the right maturity?

   a) A payout ratio that averages at least fifty percent. Yes.

4. Is expected growth reasonable?

   a) A moderate expected five-year earnings per share growth rate. No, but again in a good way. If history is any guide, more likely than not, Ross will well exceed our maximum of 12 percent.

5. Never pay too much.

   a) Value the stock correctly. Using a payout ratio of 75 percent and an average growth rate in earnings over the next 30 years of 10.0 percent, at a stock price of $95.00, and earnings per share of $4.20 – implying a current P/E ratio of 23 – the expected return is 12.3 percent a year.

TEXAS INSTRUMENTS

Texas Instruments (ticker: TXN) is a semiconductor company, a dominant player in two specialized markets: analog chips and embedded chips. The company's chips have long product life cycles and require comparatively little capital investment, enabling it to post stable long-term results. Its top three markets are industrial, personal electronics, and automotive, a particularly robust long-term driver of demand for the company's chips as vehicles continue to get accessorized with all sorts of electronic devices. In September 2018, the company announced a 24 percent increase in its annual dividend to $3.08, its 15th consecutive annual increase. Currently, the company has committed to buying back $19.4 billion of its shares, about 18 percent of its market capitalization.

Here is the checklist and my entries:

1. Does the business make sense?

    a) Stable or falling competition. Yes, with a small asterisk. Texas Instruments is the leader in analog chips and third in embedded chips. However, its market shares, 18 percent and 17 percent respectively, suggest a surfeit of players.

    b) Stable, modestly growing profits. No. Earnings per share growth has averaged 14 percent the last 10 years and growth has also been volatile – though it has looked better of late.

    c) [Ideally, share counts fall 1-2 percent a year.] Even better, exceptional, -2.9 percent a year the last 10 years. In aggregate, the number of shares has dropped 26 percent over this period.

    d) Reasonable risks. Yes, but chip stocks tend to be volatile, though the company plays in a sedate part of the chip market and the chip market has more or less matured.

2. Do the financials confirm the story?

    a) [Profit margins are good or strong.] Strong, currently, 25 percent. The 10-year average is also strong, 20 percent.

    b) Moderate financial leverage. Yes, 1.7.

    c) *A long-run return on beginning equity average of twenty percent or more.* Yes, the 10-year average is 25 percent. Currently, return on beginning equity is 35 percent.

Year	Sales	Earnings	Assets	Equity	EPS	DPS
2017	15.0	3.7	17.6	10.3	3.61	2.12
2016	13.4	3.6	16.4	10.5	3.48	1.64
2015	13.0	3.0	16.2	9.9	2.82	1.40
2014	13.0	2.8	17.7	10.4	2.57	1.24
2013	12.2	2.2	18.9	10.8	1.91	1.07
2012	12.8	1.8	20.0	11.0	1.51	0.72
2011	13.7	2.2	20.5	11.0	1.88	0.56
2010	14.0	3.2	13.4	10.4	2.62	0.49
2009	10.4	1.5	12.1	9.7	1.15	0.45
2008	12.5	1.9	11.9	9.3	1.44	0.41
2007	13.8	2.7	12.7	10.0	1.83	0.30

Table 6.16: Financial data for Texas Instruments. Numbers are in billions except for EPS (earnings per share) and DPS (dividends per share). The company's fiscal year ends in December.

3. Does the payout ratio signal the right maturity?

   a) A payout ratio that averages at least fifty percent. Yes.

4. Is expected growth reasonable?

   a) A moderate expected five-year earnings per share growth rate. Yes.

5. Never pay too much.

   a) Value the stock correctly. Using a payout ratio of 80 percent and an average growth rate in earnings over the next 30 years of 6.0 percent, at a stock price of $104.44, and earnings per share of $5.50 – implying a current P/E ratio of 19 – the expected return is 9.9 percent a year.

THE TJX COMPANIES

TJX (ticker: TJX) is the world's leading retailer of off-price apparel and home fashions. In addition to apparel stores (where it also sells home merchandise) the company has distinct home stores and has expanded overseas. The company discounts its products 20 percent to 60 percent off department and specialty store regular prices. Currently, it operates 4,194 stores in the U.S., Canada, Europe, and Australia. The company's storefronts include T.J. Maxx, Marshalls, and HomeGoods. Astonishingly, the company's comparable sales have increased 39 of the last 40 years. Long term, the company projects it can grow to 6,100 locations. The company is an aggressive buyer of its shares. In April 2018, the company announced a 25 percent increase in its annual dividend to $1.56, its 22nd consecutive annual increase. Currently, the company has committed to buying back $3.1 billion of its shares, about 5 percent of its market capitalization. The company typically announces a target amount to spend on shares each year.

Here is the checklist and my entries:

1. Does the business make sense?

   a) Stable or falling competition. Yes.

   b) Stable, modestly growing profits. No – but in (almost) a very good way. While earnings per share growth has averaged a robust 18 percent the last 10 years, earnings growth has not been stable as the company did have trouble growing earnings at the rate it had been doing in Fiscal Years 2014, 2015, and 2016. However, if recent performances are any indication, it seems to have corrected these issues.

   c) [Ideally, share counts fall 1-2 percent a year.] Even better, exceptional, -3.1 percent a year the last 10 years. In aggregate, the number of shares has dropped 27 percent over this period.

   d) Reasonable risks. Very likely. Though many retailers are now chasing the off-price concept, the company, being large and broadly diversified, is well-positioned.

2. Do the financials confirm the story?

   a) [Profit margins are good or strong.] Reasonable, currently, 7 percent. The 10-year average is also reasonable, 7 percent.

Year	Sales	Earnings	Assets	Equity	EPS	DPS
2017	35.9	2.6	14.1	5.1	4.04	1.25
2016	33.2	2.3	12.9	4.5	3.46	1.04
2015	30.9	2.3	11.5	4.3	3.33	0.84
2014	29.1	2.2	11.1	4.3	3.15	0.70
2013	27.4	2.1	10.2	4.2	2.94	0.58
2012	25.9	1.9	9.5	3.7	2.55	0.46
2011	23.2	1.5	8.3	3.2	1.93	0.38
2010	21.9	1.3	8.0	3.1	1.65	0.30
2009	20.3	1.2	7.5	2.9	1.42	0.24
2008	19.0	0.9	6.2	2.1	1.04	0.22
2007	18.3	0.8	6.6	2.1	0.84	0.18

Table 6.17: Financial data for The TJX Companies. Numbers are in billions except for EPS (earnings per share) and DPS (dividends per share). The company's fiscal year ends in January.

b) Moderate financial leverage. Yes, 2.7. The company should have no problems with this level of debt.

c) *A long-run return on beginning equity average of twenty percent or more.* Yes, the 10-year average is 53 percent. Currently, return on beginning equity is 58 percent.

3. Does the payout ratio signal the right maturity?

a) A payout ratio that averages at least fifty percent. Yes.

4. Is expected growth reasonable?

a) A moderate expected five-year earnings per share growth rate. Yes.

5. Never pay too much.

a) Value the stock correctly. Using a payout ratio of 80 percent and an average growth rate in earnings over the next 30 years of 10.0 percent, at a stock price of $97.00, and earnings per share of $5.00 – implying a current P/E ratio of 19 – the expected return is 13.4 percent a year.

THE TORO COMPANY

The Toro Company (Toro) (ticker: TTC) has been in business a long time, 104 years to be precise. Quoting from one of the company's SEC filings, they "design, manufacture, and market professional turf maintenance equipment and services, turf irrigation systems, landscaping equipment and lighting products, snow and ice management products, agricultural micro-irrigation systems, rental and specialty construction equipment, and residential yard and snow thrower products." Toro supplies professional markets, 72 percent of its business; residential markets, 27 percent; and miscellaneous, 1 percent. The company is an aggressive buyer of its shares. In December 2017, the company announced a 14 percent increase in its annual dividend to $0.80. Currently, the company has committed to buying back 2.5 million of its shares, about 2 percent of its shares outstanding.

Here is the checklist and my entries:

1. Does the business make sense?

    a) Stable or falling competition. Maybe. The company's markets look competitive. Its relatively low profit margins, while improving, confirm that.

    b) Stable, modestly growing profits. Perhaps. Earnings per share growth has averaged 14 percent the last 10 years, in line with the target that we look for in more robust midsize dividend growth companies. However, growth can be volatile, a reflection of its underlying markets.

    c) [Ideally, share counts fall 1-2 percent a year.] Even better, exceptional, -3.6 percent a year the last 10 years. In aggregate, the number of shares has dropped 30 percent over this period.

    d) Reasonable risks. Yes, though competitve markets (as proof, the lowish profit margins) are not fun. The company is a midcap. The company did not raise its dividend in 2009, likely a result of the Crash of 2008's economic consequences.

2. Do the financials confirm the story?

    a) [Profit margins are good or strong.] Good, currently, 11 percent. The 10-year average is reasonable, 7 percent.

    b) Moderate financial leverage. Maybe, 2.4.

Year	Sales	Earnings	Assets	Equity	EPS	DPS
2017	2505	268	1494	617	2.41	0.70
2016	2392	231	1385	550	2.06	0.60
2015	2391	202	1192	409	1.78	0.50
2014	2173	174	1003	359	1.51	0.40
2013	2041	155	871	267	1.31	0.28
2012	1959	130	886	276	1.07	0.22
2011	1884	118	871	267	0.93	0.20
2010	1690	93	886	276	0.70	0.18
2009	1523	63	873	315	0.43	0.15
2008	1878	120	932	365	0.78	0.15
2007	1877	142	951	370	0.85	0.12

Table 6.18: Financial data for The Toro Corporation. Numbers are in millions except for EPS (earnings per share) and DPS (dividends per share). The company's fiscal year ends in October.

c) *A long-run return on beginning equity average of twenty percent or more.* Yes, the 10-year average is 45 percent. Currently, return on beginning equity is 49 percent.

3. Does the payout ratio signal the right maturity?

a) A payout ratio that averages at least fifty percent. Yes.

4. Is expected growth reasonable?

a) A moderate expected five-year earnings per share growth rate. Yes. As a more robust midsize dividend growth company, Toro should be able to average more than 12 percent earnings per share growth the next five years.

5. Never pay too much.

a) Value the stock correctly. Using a payout ratio of 80 percent and an average growth rate in earnings over the next 30 years of 10.0 percent, at a stock price of $60.00, and earnings per share of $2.65 – implying a current P/E ratio of 23 – the expected return is 12.7 percent a year.

THE STOCK MARKET

The stock market has been on an absolute tear since bottoming in March 2009, having risen more than 410 percent, including reinvested dividends, off that bottom, as of mid-2018.

However, as with *all* long bull markets, the market invariably becomes overvalued as the gains in stock prices outpace the gains in fundamentals (essentially because of investor overconfidence, investors continually buying, having watched the market rise for so long, and getting accustomed to prices continually going up). Consequently, the market's P/E ratio keeps ratcheting higher.

Eventually, however, the stock market reaches a point where it simply cannot, and will not, rise any further. Next, there comes some event, typically out of the blue, to trigger the selling – and once the selling starts it cascades, taking stock prices down *far* faster than it took for them to rise, the increased investor leverage in long-running bull markets helping not at all in this regard.

Let's see if we can use our magic formula to benchmark and value the stock market. In the aggregate, I'll take the liberty of assuming that the stock market is one big dividend growth stock, as customarily defined. After all, over the long term, dividends (per share) and earnings per share have grown about 6.5 percent a year. With a share buyback effect of about 1.0 percentage points a year, the earnings growth rate is 5.5 percent a year. Also over the long term, and also in the aggregate, companies have spent about 60 percent of their earnings on share buybacks and dividends, with, in recent years, the percentage spent on share buybacks rising and the percentage spent on dividends falling. We cannot quite assume this 60 percent is the market's payout ratio because some buybacks are supported by debt, and more importantly this 60 percent excludes the cash contribution from shares issued. With some hesitation, I will guesstimate a payout ratio of 55 percent. I will use the Standard & Poor's® 500 stock index as the proxy for the market.

As of 31 August 2018, according to Standard & Poor's, the Standard & Poor's® 500 stock index had a trailing P/E ratio of 22.9 and a forward P/E ratio of 17.3. As I prefer to use earnings per share six months in the past plus six months in the future, I will use a current P/E ratio of (22.9 + 17.3) / 2 or 20.1, rounded to 20. This P/E ratio is still biased to the upside because of the recent corporate tax cut, but, for now, I will let this be. (Realistically, something lower, like 18, might be better. Also, in my opinion, the P/E ratio poses another general problem because with some stocks, such as cyclicals, a high P/E ratio does not necessarily signal over-valuation. Few investors seem to appreciate this. Theoretically, the P/E ratio *must* be adjusted. This, I will ignore, if for no other reason than to get some comparability with what others do. Finally, the E in the P/E ratio is not always consistently calculated, another reason why calculations – and conclusions – often differ.)

Let's benchmark the index first. From Table 5.1, on page 97, the canonical dividend growth stock's expected return, given a current P/E ratio of 20, is 10.3 percent. Given that the index in no way matches the quality of our canonical dividend growth stock – almost by definition – I'd say the index is worse than the canonical dividend growth stock and, over the long term, should therefore return less than 10.3 percent a year, a not too earth-shattering conclusion since the market has historically returned between 9 percent and 10 percent a year.

Next, let's value the index. Because average growth rate in earnings is 2.5 percentage points lower than the canonical dividend growth stock's, decrease the canonical dividend growth stock's expected return 2.5 * 0.9 percentage points, or 2.3 percentage points. Because payout ratio is 10 percentage points lower than the canonical dividend growth stock's, decrease the expected return 2 * 0.4 percentage points, or 0.8 percentage points. Thus, because the canonical dividend growth stock's return is 10.3 percent, the index is expected to return 10.3 - 2.3 - 0.8 percent, or 7.2 percent a year, definitely on the weak side of history, and not surprising considering how long this bull market has persisted.

Let's do a quick consistency check. The market's average current P/E ratio is about 14. The canonical dividend growth stock's expected return, given a current P/E ratio of 14, is 12.4 percent, 2.1 percentage points higher than that calculated with a current P/E ratio of 20. In turn, this implies that the market will return 2.1 percentage points more than the 7.2 percent calculated in the previous paragraph, or 9.3 percent, in line with historical levels. Thus, we are probably in the right ballpark with our current estimation.

As noted, the recent corporate tax cut is biasing the current P/E ratio. So, instead of 20, let's assume an "adjusted" current P/E ratio of 18. In this case, the index's expected return rises to 7.7 percent a year, still on the weak side of history.

Vanguard Dividend Appreciation ETF

The Vanguard Dividend Appreciation ETF "tracks the performance of the NASDAQ US Dividend Achievers Select Index, which consists of common stocks of companies that have a record of increasing dividends over time." In effect, this ETF is a proxy for the market's, but not our, definition of a dividend growth stock.

Let's benchmark and value this ETF, at least roughly. As of 31 July 2018, the ETF had a *trailing* P/E ratio of 24, a return on equity of 20 percent, and in the last five years, an earnings per share growth rate of just 3 percent (ouch!). This last number is likely not adjusted. Because of the recent corporate tax cut, the current P/E ratio is biased. Something closer to 22, at the very least, might be better. Something like 21 might be even better, but let's be conservative. Let us assume a reasonable payout ratio of 70 percent. For earnings per share, a more reasonable adjusted value might be 8 percent. With 1.5 percentage points due to share buybacks, the earnings growth rate is 6.5 percent.

Let's benchmark the ETF first. From Table 5.1, on page 97, the canonical dividend growth stock's expected return, given a current P/E ratio of 22, is 9.8 percent. Given the ETF's lower return on equity and lower earnings growth rate, the ETF is worse than the canonical dividend growth stock. Thus, over the long term, it should therefore return less than 9.8 percent a year.

Next, let's value the ETF. Because average growth rate in earnings is 1.5 percentage points lower than the canonical dividend growth stock's, decrease the canonical dividend growth stock's expected return 1.5 * 0.9 percentage points, or 1.4 percentage points. Because payout ratio is 5 percentage points higher than the canonical dividend growth stock's, increase the expected return 0.4 percentage points. Thus, because the canonical dividend growth stock's return is 9.8 percent, the ETF is expected to return 9.8 - 1.4 + 0.4 percent, or 8.8 percent a year. This return meshes reasonably well with the ETF's return of 8.2 percent a year since inception, April 2006. So we are probably in the right ballpark. (Remember, the return since inception included the Crash of 2008, which of course decimated returns.) An expected return of 8.8 percent a year is relatively low for this ETF over the long term.

APPENDIX – FIGURING OUT THE PAYOUT RATIO

"As far as the laws of mathematics refer to reality, they are not certain, and as far as they are certain, they do not refer to reality." Albert Einstein

Figuring out the payout ratio is not easy! Here, I detail the steps I took to estimate a reasonable payout ratio for Texas Instruments.

(This appendix requires a healthy understanding of some accounting terms. It is also fairly complicated. If you are not comfortable with these concepts, or are simply not in the mood for this sort of stuff, feel free to skip.)

I start with 10 years of the company's cash flow statements. A company's cash flow consists of (a) the cash generated by its operations (operating cash flow); (b) the cash (usually) used in investments such as property and equipment (investing cash flow); and (c) the cash for financing the company's business (financing cash flow). Dividends, share buybacks, and share issuances appear in financing cash flow.

Table 6.19 summarizes Texas Instruments' operating cash flow for 2008-2017. Likewise, Tables 6.20 and 6.21 summarize the company's investing and financing cash flow over the same period. I assembled this data from Texas Instruments' investor relations website, where the company has a 10-year financial summary, and the SEC website.

What I aim to do with all these numbers is eventually get to something like this:

$$XYZ \text{ of earnings} \quad = \quad ABC \text{ of dividends and share buybacks, net}$$
$$+ \quad DEF \text{ of investments}$$
$$+ \quad GHI \text{ of change in cash and cash-equivalents}$$

Then, with some qualifications, ABC divided by XYZ is the payout ratio that I am after. In this equation, *net* means cash spent on share buybacks *minus* cash received from shares issued.

The basic premise is that when a company generates earnings, it, in turn, returns money to shareholders in the form of dividends and share buybacks or makes investments (which will in time generate more earnings) or retains cash, either for a rainy day or as a natural

Year	OCF	Earnings	DA	IWC	Other OCF
2017	5363	3682	904	418	359
2016	4614	3595	955	153	-89
2015	4397	2986	1133	140	138
2014	4054	2821	1230	-161	164
2013	3514	2162	1297	-232	287
2012	3483	1759	1401	297	26
2011	3334	2236	1108	-221	211
2010	3839	3228	1005	-253	-141
2009	2647	1470	1013	-15	179
2008	3352	1920	1153	306	-27
Total	38597	25859	11199	432	1107

Table 6.19: Texas Instruments: 10-Year Operating Cash Flow Summary. OCF is operating cash flow. DA is depreciation & amortization. IWC is investments in working capital. Financial data are in millions.

Year	ICF	IFC, net	Acquisitions	STI, net purchases	Other ICF
2017	-1127	-655	0	-460	-12
2016	-650	-531	0	-113	-6
2015	-302	-441	0	125	14
2014	-377	-243	0	-141	7
2013	-3	-391	0	342	46
2012	-1039	-495	0	-604	60
2011	-6172	-800	-5425	-98	151
2010	-1057	-1051	-199	54	139
2009	-1096	-753	-155	-243	55
2008	-1182	-763	-19	-446	46
Total	-13005	-6123	-5798	-1584	500

Table 6.20: Texas Instruments: 10-Year Investing Cash Flow Summary. ICF is investing cash flow. IFC is investments in fixed capital. STI is short-term investments. Financial data are in millions.

Year	FinCF	Dividends	SB, Net	LTD, net proceeds	Other FinCF
2017	-3734	-2104	-2073	474	-31
2016	-3810	-1646	-1660	-501	-3
2015	-4294	-1444	-2345	-502	-3
2014	-3943	-1323	-2277	-502	159
2013	-3170	-1175	-1604	-514	123
2012	-1951	-819	-1308	117	59
2011	2589	-644	-1330	4497	66
2010	-2626	-592	-2053	0	19
2009	-1411	-567	-848	0	4
2008	-2430	-537	-1915	0	22
Total	-24780	-10851	-17413	3069	415

Table 6.21: Texas Instruments: 10-Year Financing Cash Flow Summary. FinCF is financing cash flow. SB is share buybacks. LTD is long-term debt. Financial data are in millions.

necessity as the business grows. (There's also the problem of companies retaining more cash than they should.)

Figure 6.1 shows how I arrive at this equation for Texas Instruments – where the change in cash over the 10 years is $812 (million) and is not shown in the earlier tables – thereby also arriving at an estimate of the company's payout ratio, the ultimate goal. In the figure, the abbreviations refer to the same abbreviations as in the earlier tables. One more point, as with all such calculations, I consider short-term investments to be cash equivalents. As the figure shows, with a dose of conservatism, I estimate a payout ratio for Texas Instruments of 80 percent.

An alternative, and often far simpler, approach to developing the payout ratio – though not nearly as revealing – is to utilize the sustainable growth rate idea and start from return on beginning equity and subtract earnings growth. Table 6.22 shows the return on beginning equity data that I use. Once again, I start with a long period, generally ten years, then simply calculate each year's return on beginning equity and take the average. Many companies, Texas Instruments included, have shown a strong jump in return on beginning equity in recent years, at least partly the result of low interest rates. However, *being conservative in the interest of long-term valuations*, though granted

Start with:

OCF + ICF + FinCF = Change in Cash

But:

OCF = Earnings + DA + IWC + Other OCF
ICF = (IFC, net + Acquisitions) + STI, net purchases + Other ICF
FinCF = (Dividends + SB, net) + LTD, net proceeds + Other FinCF

Substituting these in the first equation and rearranging:

Earnings =

-(Dividends + SB, net)
-(IFC, net + Acquisitions + DA + IWC)
+(Change in Cash - STI, net purchases)
- LTD, net proceeds
-(Other OCF + Other ICF + Other FinCF)

Putting in the values for Texas Instruments over the last 10 years:

25859 = 28264 + 290 + 2396 - 3069 - 2022

The first three terms on the right are what I am after.

The two negative terms are a problem. One may allocate them
proportionately or, in this case, not so proportionately, or do something else.
I choose to reduce the first term. In effect, I am saying the company's return
to shareholders was aided by these two ("unusual", "fictitious") numbers,
so I will take these off.

Thus:

25859 = 23173 + 290 + 2396

This is what I am after. The payout ratio is thus, 23173 / 25859, or 90 percent.
(Of the remaining 10 percent, 1 percent was allocated to investing
and 9 percent was retained in cash and short-term investments.)

Here, the investments look much too low to me. I tend to be more conservative,
and typically tack on more for investing, in this case, about 10 percentage points.

With this adjustment, the payout ratio drops from 90 percent to 80 percent.

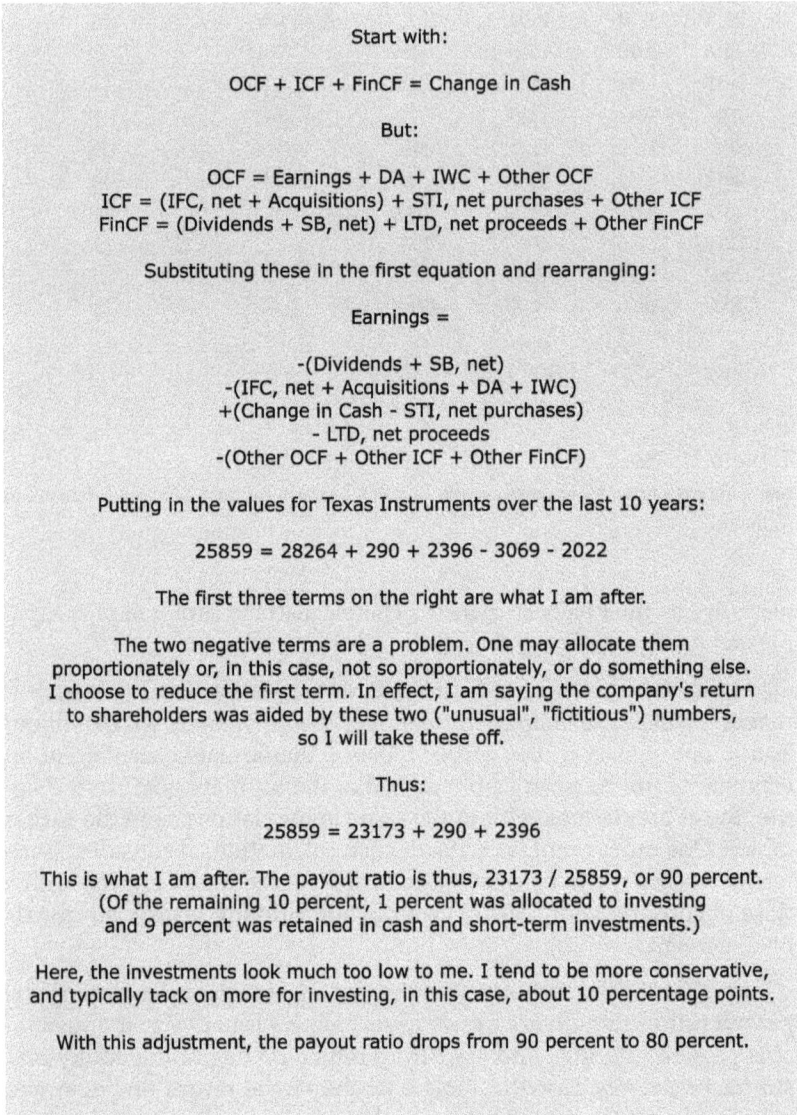

Figure 6.1: Determining the payout ratio for Texas Instruments from cash flow.

Year	Earnings	Beginning Equity	RoBE	Earnings Growth
2017	3682	10473	35%	2%
2016	3595	9946	36%	20%
2015	2986	10390	29%	6%
2014	2821	10807	26%	30%
2013	2162	10961	20%	23%
2012	1759	10952	16%	-21%
2011	2236	10437	21%	-31%
2010	3228	9722	33%	120%
2009	1470	9326	16%	-23%
2008	1920	9975	19%	-28%
2007	2657			
Average			25%	10%

Table 6.22: Texas Instruments: 10-Year Return on Beginning Equity and Earnings Growth. RoBE is return on beginning equity. Earnings and beginning equity are in millions.

perhaps excessively so here, I will use the 25 percent.

(Realize also that these numbers do not take into account the generous corporate tax cut enacted in 2018, which for a company like Texas Instruments, bumps up the return on beginning equity another 2-4 percentage points depending on which long-term value you wish to start out with. It's the real deal.)

Table 6.22 also shows the company's earnings growth, simply much too volatile for me to have much faith in the average. Normally, I would then try a trend line but I believe the data is just too jagged to get anything of value. A fancier approach uses adjusted earnings but that can be quite complicated. So let's just stop. That's the real world for you! (Also remember that using this approach does require that the company actually operate at its maximum, or close to it, not far below it or far above it. With quite a few companies, this is not always easy to achieve. Still, this approach often provides a reasonable validation check to the primary cash flow approach.)

NOTES

- Companies do have an obligation to pay their shareholders, ideally, as with our select dividend growth companies, maintaining a good, stable, moderate long-term growth rate in the process as well. An excellent read, though it does use some accounting terminology, which you can gloss over, from one of our companies, Texas Instruments, on their capital management strategy, *https://goo.gl/hUFzgT*

- Once a company has paid its dividend, these dividends *definitely* do matter to your return. Many news outlets and authors, however, fail to include dividends when calculating returns. For instance, while I calculated a return of more than 410 percent, many outlets displayed a considerably lower return, the difference seemingly because the authors neglected dividends. To calculate returns for the Standard & Poor's® 500 stock index with dividends included, look up historical prices for the S&P 500 Total Return Index (^SP500TR) on Yahoo! Finance and use the Adjusted Close column: *https://goo.gl/Y4g1aj*

- More on the bull market's rise since the bottom on March 9, 2009: *https://goo.gl/kPnX7z*

- Payout ratio of no more than 60 percent for the stock market (this 60 percent does not account for cash from shares issued and cash from debt used to buy back shares): *https://goo.gl/v8fWws*

- P/Es and dividend yields on major indexes, from the *Wall Street Journal*: *https://goo.gl/G5TwAC*

- Standard & Poor's® 500 stock index, *https://goo.gl/bZrdnM*. The associated factsheet on this webpage has the index P/E ratio, both trailing and projected.

- Portfolio characteristics of the Vanguard Dividend Appreciation ETF: *https://goo.gl/L6aWT3* ♣

Dividend Growth Whisperer

"Well, that was fun. Now for eons of loneliness."
Bender (Futurama)

(1) The business matters. First, ask: What is the competition?

(2) Stability matters: Look for stable, modestly growing profits.

(3) Quality matters: A long-run return on beginning equity of at least twenty percent – with no more than reasonable financial leverage.

(4) Maturity matters: A payout ratio that averages at least fifty percent.

(5) The future matters: An expected five-year earnings per share growth rate of 8-12 percent a year for large companies and 8-16 percent a year for midsize ones.

(6) Valuation matters – I: The magic formula (or, Table 5.1 on page 97) for our canonical dividend growth stock :

$$-0.000828 * p^3 + 0.0625 * p^2 - 1.75 * p + 26.9$$

(7) Valuation matters – II: For our canonical dividend growth stock, roughly, in the context of historical stock market returns, a current P/E ratio of 15 or lower is excellent (generating a 12 percent, or higher, return), 21 is reasonable (a 10 percent return), and 26 or higher is pricey (a 9 percent, or lower, return). Rough modifications for other dividend growth stocks: For each percentage point higher in average growth rate in earnings over the next 30 years, increase the expected return 0.90 percentage points. For each 5 percentage points of the payout ratio higher than 65 percent, increase the expected return 0.40 percentage points. In both cases, lower values work the opposite way, generating decreases.

Epilogue

"And that's the way it is."

Walter Cronkite

This book began with the simple conviction that, before anything else, *the business matters*, with the degree of *competitive pressure* being the most important clue. In turn, the necessary qualitative business traits led naturally to the *numerical proof* necessary to confirm that the business is indeed of high quality, namely, that it *consistently* sports a *return on beginning equity, a type of internal return, of more than 20 percent* (with a reasonable level of debt). Throw in a *moderately growing underlying market* and *profits will be stable and modestly growing* as well. Moreover, this high of an internal return *virtually guarantees* that the company can not only make the necessary investments to support the business but also comfortably pay a reasonable and rising dividend, supplementing the dividend with share buybacks if it so chooses – the net result for our dividend growth stocks being a *payout ratio of at least 50 percent*. The simplest way to find such stocks? Peek at the *holdings* of well-run dividend growth mutual funds and ETFs or *screen* if you are willing to put in more work. Finally, we needed a relatively simple way to gauge how much to pay, that is, effectively, we needed to know how to *value* our dividend growth stocks. That's where the *magic formula*, or the *associated table*, and the two *heuristics*, come in. Put it all together and we have a strong and logically complete system that, if we get our assumptions right, virtually guarantees long-term investing success.

With these stocks, the math – from business to stock market to investor – simply works. Everything fits, maximizing your return. With most other stocks, the math does not work – something along the line breaks. That's the crux of it.

Contrary to what many pundits, including many academics, say, picking high-quality stocks, in particular, our high-quality dividend growth stocks, is not difficult – or impossible. This is not black art. Instead, you just need to think clearly, keep the right temperament, and thoroughly appreciate the key points in this book, especially those of the checklist.

And, yes, you can, perhaps comfortably even, beat the market (over the long term) – if you invest in the right stocks, for most investors, our high-quality dividend growth stocks being, in my opinion, the best category of long-term choices. As long as you understand the ideas in this book well, apply them carefully, and remain patient over the time frame necessary to build substantial wealth, you should do fine.

Good luck! ♣ ♣

Recommended Reading

"Nothing in this world is so powerful as an idea whose time has come."   *Victor Hugo*

The following three investment classics cover the essentials of good businesses and good stocks.

> **Philip A. Fisher,** *Common Stocks and Uncommon Profits and Other Writings*, 2nd edition (John Wiley & Sons, 2003).

> **Benjamin Graham,** *The Intelligent Investor: A book of practical counsel*, 4th edition (Harper & Row Publishers, 1986).

> **Peter Lynch and John Rothchild,** *One Up On Wall Street: How to use what you already know to make money in the market*, 2nd edition (Simon & Schuster, 2000).

The next book covers screening.

> **Michael Kaye,** *The Standard & Poor's Guide to Selecting Stocks: Finding the Winners & Weeding out the Losers* (McGraw-Hill Education, 2005).

The final four books cover dividends. Carrel offers a comprehensive approach. My two books offer a complete theory and practical application of dividend growth – the digital edition being an updated and substantially enlarged version of the print edition. As a dividend-focused investor, you will find Peters' Chapters 6 ("Is it Safe?"), 7 ("Will it Grow?"), and 8 ("What's the Return?") useful.

> **Lawrence Carrel,** *Dividend Stocks For Dummies* (Wiley Publishing, 2010).

> **Shane Forbes,** *Investing in Dividend Growth Stocks: A Safer More Realistic Path to Financial Freedom* (print edition, NeoCadence LLC, 2015).

> **Shane Forbes,** *Investing in Dividend Growth Stocks: A Safer More Realistic Path to Financial Freedom* (digital edition, NeoCadence LLC, 2017).

> **Josh Peters and Morningstar,** *The Ultimate Dividend Playbook: Income, insight and independence for today's investor* (John Wiley & Sons, 2008).

Tickers

Yahoo! Finance tickers, as of mid-2018.

3M	MMM
Abbott	ABT
ABM Industries	ABM
Accenture	ACN
Aflac	AFL
Air Products and Chemicals	APD
Albemarle	ALB
Amphenol	APH
Analog Devices	ADI
Becton Dickinson	BDX

Berkshire Hathaway	BRK-A
Berkshire Hathaway	BRK-B
Brown-Forman	BF-A
Brown-Forman	BF-B
Bunge	BG
Carlisle	CSL
Church & Dwight	CHD
Cincinnati Financial	CINF
Cintas	CTAS
Cisco	CSCO
Clorox	CLX
Coca-Cola	KO
Colgate-Palmolive	CL
Costco	COST
CVS Health	CVS
Donaldson Company	DCI
Dover	DOV
Ecolab	ECL
Emerson Electric	EMR
Erie Indemnity	ERIE
FactSet	FDS
Fannie Mae	FNMA
Ford	F
Franklin Rising Dividends Fund (Class A Shares)	FRDPX
Freddie Mac	FMCC
General Dynamics	GD
General Electric	GE
Genuine Parts	GPC
Graco	GGG
Grainger (W. W.)	GWW
Home Depot	HD
Honeywell	HON
IBM	IBM
Illinois Tool Works	ITW
Intel	INTC
John Wiley & Sons	JW-B
Johnson & Johnson	JNJ

Kimberly-Clark	KMB
Las Vegas Sands	LVS
Lockheed Martin	LMT
Lowe's	LOW
Matthews	MATW
McCormick	MKC
McDonald's	MCD
Medtronic	MDT
Microsoft	MSFT
NASDAQ US Dividend Achievers^{TM} Select Index	^DVG
Netflix	NFLX
Nike	NKE
Nokia	NOK
Nucor	NUE
Oracle	ORCL
Paccar	PCAR
Papa John's	PZZA
Parker-Hannifin	PH
PepsiCo	PEP
Perrigo	PRGO
Praxair	PX
Roper	ROP
Ross Stores	ROST
Stanley Black & Decker	SWK
Stryker	SYK
T. Rowe Price Dividend Growth Fund	PRDGX
Target	TGT
Texas Instruments	TXN
Tiffany	TIF
TJX Companies, The	TJX
Toro Company, The	TTC
Union Pacific	UNP
United Technologies	UTX

Vanguard Dividend Appreciation ETF	VIG
Vanguard Dividend Appreciation Index Fund Investor Shares	VDAIX
Walgreens Boots Alliance	WBA
Walmart	WMT
West Pharmaceutical Services	WST

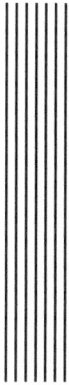

Glossary

asset turnover ratio *see efficiency*

assets items, tangible or not, that a company owns or controls and which can be expected to produce benefits in the future

balance sheet a snapshot of a company's assets, debt, and equity at the end of a reporting period

beta a gauge of risk relative to the market, measured by how much a stock moves relative to the market

buyback *see share buyback*

capital gain an increase in the value of an asset

capital loss a decrease in the value of an asset

cash flow difference between money flowing into the business and money flowing out

debt portion of assets owned by non-shareholders, more commonly referred to as liabilities elsewhere

dividend growth a category of stocks ideally suited for long-term investors, also a synonym for growth rate in dividends, the dividend growth rate

dividend growth stocks your best long-term investment, allowing you to sleep better *and* get wealthier at the same time, usually faster than with the general stock market

dividend payout ratio dividends per share divided by earnings per share, or, more carefully, (total) dividends divided by (total) earnings

dividend per share total dividends paid out by the company divided by the number of shares outstanding

dividend reinvestment a strategy of using a company's dividends to automatically buy more shares in the company

dividend yield equivalent annual dividend, that is, current dividend annualized, divided by current stock price

dividends distributions that companies make to their shareholders, typically in cash

earnings what a company earns for its shareholders, also known as profits, the difference between sales and the various costs and expenses to make those sales

earnings per share earnings divided by the number of shares outstanding, often abbreviated to eps

efficiency sales divided by assets, more commonly referred to as asset turnover ratio elsewhere

eps *see earnings per share*

equity portion of assets owned by shareholders

financial leverage assets divided by equity

growth formally, the change in value of some quantity, so, for example, the value of that quantity now minus the value of that quantity a year earlier, often used interchangeably with growth rate

growth in eps commonly used term for growth rate in earnings per share

growth rate change in the value of a quantity divided by the starting value of the quantity

income statement a record of a company's sales during a period and a demonstration of how, after deductions, these sales are transformed into earnings

large-cap a company whose market capitalization is between $10 billion and $199.9 billion (applicable at the time of writing of this book)

magic formula a formula from this book that makes accurately valuing dividend growth stocks a piece of cake

market capitalization share price times number of shares outstanding, a measure of how large a company is in the stock market

megacap a company whose market capitalization is $200 billion or more (applicable at the time of writing of this book)

microcap a company whose market capitalization is less than $300 million (applicable at the time of writing of this book)

midcap a company whose market capitalization is between $2 billion and $9.9 billion (applicable at the time of writing of this book)

P/E ratio price per share (P) divided by earnings per share (E)

P/S ratio price per share (P) divided by sales per share (S)

payout ratio a modification of the dividend payout ratio, where instead of dividends we add cash spent on share buybacks, subtract cash received from shares issued, and include additional cash that a company can return to shareholders but for whatever reason does not

PEG ratio P/E ratio divided by earnings per share growth rate (G) in percentage points, popularized by Peter Lynch

PEYG ratio P/E ratio divided by the sum of dividend yield (Y) and earnings per share growth rate (G), both in percentage points

portfolio a collection of stocks and other assets

profit margin earnings divided by sales, also referred to as net profit margin

profits *see earnings*

return a measure of how well an investment has performed

return on beginning equity earnings divided by beginning equity

return on equity earnings divided by equity

risk related to the uncertainty of knowing what the future price of a stock will be

share buyback when a company buys back its shares, typically directly in the stock market, but also privately and through other means

small-cap a company whose market capitalization is between $300 million and $1.9 billion (applicable at the time of writing of this book)

stability of a quantity, relatively low volatility

stock representing ownership in a business, more accurately referred to as common stock elsewhere

stock market a market where buyers and sellers trade stocks

sustainable growth rate how fast a company can grow without raising net new funds from shareholders

valuation a method of valuing a stock, here, a process to infer the return implied by the current stock price

volatility a measure of the unpredictability of a stock price or other quantity

Index

www.ingramcontent.com/pod-product-compliance
Lightning Source LLC
Chambersburg PA
CBHW020201200326
41521CB00005BA/214